"Thanks for your delightful book. It is supe. wisdom of a lifetime's experiences, observations and analysis. Practical, appealing, encouraging and warm, your concise work helps your readers navigate the complexities of communication with clarity and humor."

—Henry Gibson, Actor

◼ ◼ ◼

"Hundreds of librarians have seen and heard Arch at conferences. Hundreds more have seen his tapes. And this book distills the proven, easily remembered Lustberg tips for effective public speaking, convincing presentations and handling interviews.

—Charles W. Robinson, Director Emeritus,
Baltimore County Public Library;
Editor, *Library Administrator's Digest*

◼ ◼ ◼

"Nervous speakers have long been advised to 'picture the audience naked' as a tool for overcoming stage fright. For the truly professional speaker, however, Arch Lustberg reveals far more useful—and practical—techniques for giving effective, engaging presentations in his book."

—*Spectrum: The Journal of State Government*

◼ ◼ ◼

"The essence of acting is the ability to guide and control the thoughts and emotions of the audience. The speaker is the first cousin of the actor, sharing the need to reach an audience's heart and mind. To help you achieve that, I recommend the expert advice of Arch Lustberg."

—Philip Bosco, Actor

ARCH LUSTBERG

HOW TO

SELL YOURSELF

REVISED EDITION

◻

Using Leadership, Likability, *and* Luck to Succeed

 CAREER
PRESS
Franklin Lakes, NJ

HOW TO SELL YOURSELF, REVISED EDITION
EDITED BY JODI BRANDON
TYPESET BY EILEEN DOW MUNSON
Photographs by W.A. Williams
Cover design by Lu Rossman/Digi Dog Design NY
Printed in the U.S.A. by Book-mart Press

TelePrompTer® is a registered trademark.
United States Chamber of Commerce Communicator® is a registered trademark.

To order this title, please call toll-free 1-800-CAREER-1 (NJ and Canada: 201-848-0310) to order using VISA or MasterCard, or for further information on books from Career Press.

The Career Press, Inc., 3 Tice Road, PO Box 687,
Franklin Lakes, NJ 07417
www.careerpress.com

Library of Congress Cataloging-in-Publication Data
Lustberg, Arch.
    How to sell yourself : using leadership, likability, and luck to succeed / by Arch Lustberg. — Rev. ed.
        p. cm.
    Includes index.
    ISBN 978-1-56414-998-5
        1. Interpersonal communication. 2. Success. I. Title.

BF637.C45L877 2008
153.6--dc22

                                                        2007046870

■ ■ ■

For Hunter,
Liam,
and
Jackson

■

Enjoy,
Arch Lustberg

Acknowledgments

This book would not be a reality without the help of three of the key women in my life: Marguerite Savard, who runs my business; Susan Paynter Hasankulizade, who edits my quarterly newsletter; and my wife, Jean Anne, whose five published novels were part of my literary training.

And I mustn't forget Robert Patrick O'Connor, the editor who made all of Jean Anne's and all of my books happen.

Contents

Introduction

Communication is the transfer of information from one mind to another mind, or to a group of other minds. It can be in the form of an idea, a fact, an image, an emotion, or a story. It can be written, spoken, drawn, danced, sung, or mimed.

Whatever the medium, if the message doesn't reach the other person, there's no communication, or there's miscommunication.

The simple premise of this book is that every time you open your mouth, in order for communication to happen, you have to sell yourself. If you don't sell yourself, communication is nearly impossible. If you do, your message will get across.

We think of selling as being product-oriented. But that's only one aspect of selling. In the case of product sales, the governing factors are usually the salesperson and the price. Even when there's a slight price difference, we rarely buy any big-ticket item from someone we really dislike.

Ideas aren't much different. The only time we pay close attention to an idea being communicated by someone we don't like is when we have a heavy personal or emotional investment in the subject.

I grew up in prehistoric times when ice was delivered by a man in a wagon. Frigidaire was the generic name for electric and gas "ice boxes" because it was the *only* one. There was no television. Think of it—*no television!* Phone calls were made by calling an operator. Most public transportation cost a nickel. So did a Coke. Underage smart-aleck kids could buy "loosies," single cigarettes, at a penny apiece. What there was of an upper middle class could buy a new car for $500. That was big bucks then. That was the time when the voice was the critical communication tool. Radio was the mass-communication medium. The political candidate boomed his message from the rear observation car of the train. Then, without warning, the Industrial Revolution evolved into the technological revolution.

Today, everyone around us seems to be carrying a personal, palm-sized telephone and message center. The Blackberry, the iPhone, and all their clones, along with the laptop computer, are almost required pieces of carry-on luggage. The beeper makes civilized conversation nearly impossible. It seems that nothing is out of technological reach. I.T.—Information Technology—is all the rage, whereas person-to-person communication is rapidly going out of style.

This was brought home to me in spades in October 2006. Elliot Masie, a leading expert in the Information Technology field, invited me to present at his annual conference. It was called "Leadership 2006." Nearly 2,000 corporate, government, and trade and professional association thought leaders attended. Elliot brought me in to introduce them to the nearly forgotten subject of face-to-face communication. The keyboard, monitor, fax, e-mail, the aforementioned handheld message center—all tremendously valuable tools—have conspired to make spoken communication obsolete.

But somehow, there has never been anything to replace the hand-shake, the hug, and the "hello." Face-to-face communication is still, and is likely always to be, irreplaceable. Whether it's one-on-one or one with a group, the personal touch is a powerhouse.

The keyboard will never be a complete substitute for the human face, body, and voice. Yes, the machine can take us into new adventures, but if it ever actually replaces our interpersonal relationships, we will have become machines ourselves. Robots. Mechanical replicas of human beings. Elliot told me that my session was so well received that he invited me back the next year to present at "Learning 2007."

The child in school won't become a better person because there's a computer at every desk in the classroom. Loving, caring, giving, sharing parents, teachers, and administrators will always produce a better-quality next generation. A mouse will never replace a mom. Not even a Disney mouse.

There was a time when I believed that teleconferencing would put airlines and hotels out of business. I'd have bet money on it. I wasn't thinking straight. In fact, not even the horrendous September 11, 2001, disaster could stop people from wanting to "work the crowd" at meetings, conventions, seminars, and retreats. I'm more convinced than ever that it's even more important that we do some essential things together. In the same room. At the same time. Networking in the form of personal contact will never go out of style.

Many companies that decided to save money by selling to old customers via phone, fax, and modem soon realized that their sales and bottom lines were getting killed by the competitor who kept the sales force in the field calling on the client. Whether it takes place in the office, over a meal, on the golf course, or at a gathering, "hands on" is the final arbiter in a lot of situations. And don't forget: Candidates for public office are still pounding the pavement, knocking on doors, and pressing the flesh. No question about it: Television commercials are still considered the key to getting elected, but the candidates have never stopped going door-to-door, to the factory gate, the bus or subway stop, the diner, and every place else people congregate.

Don't get me wrong. I'm not bad-mouthing technology. It's certainly taking the world by storm, and it has only just begun.

As the early pioneers of the automobile couldn't conceive of jet travel in the air, we're ignorant of what's ahead 20 years from now. Ideas that took thousands of years to become reality are achievable in seconds.

The danger is that, as we become more sophisticated at the keyboard, we're becoming almost helpless communicating by mouth.

I'm not unaware of the success of shop-at-home programs, interactive television, and those jobs that eliminate the chore of commuting and allow people to work out of their own homes. But pretty soon all of us feel a need to make contact with another real, live, adult human being. Companionship is an idea that will never go out of style.

That brings me to the substance of this book. The more dependent we become on the new age of technology, the higher the speed limit goes on the information superhighway, the more bytes it takes to digest a feast of facts, figures, and statistics, the more pressing will be our need to speak well.

After all, every time you open your mouth to speak, you're doing the equivalent of selling yourself, whether the communication is:

- Exchanging a greeting.
- Talking on the phone.
- Chatting with family, friends, colleagues, strangers, or clients.
- Speaking up at a meeting.
- Delivering a presentation.
- Interviewing for a job.
- Running as a candidate for election.
- Testifying before a legislative or regulatory body, or a jury.
- Teaching.
- Preaching.
- Negotiating.

That's what selling yourself is all about. It's getting your message across, sending the right signals that you're saying what you mean and that you mean what you say. Understanding you should take no special effort on the part of the person to whom you're talking.

Today, it seems as though everything is conspiring to make us do the wrong things. When I opened my business years ago, my first call was from the Yellow Pages. The representative told me I was entitled to a free listing. I asked what my options were and got six or seven categories. I picked the one I thought was perfect. I chose "Communications Consultant." Today, I'm getting calls to fix fax machines. Technology has taken over and replaced the real person.

It's become frustrating to call a company that depends on customers for business. This is what we're hearing more often than not:

"This call may be recorded to ensure quality.

Please listen carefully as our menu has changed.

If you are calling to...press 1.

For information about...,press 2.

If you want to report a..., press 3.

If you know your party's extension, press it now.

For other reasons not covered, please stay on the line.

All our operators are currently serving other customers.

Your call is important to us, so please stay on the line."

Two minutes later...

"Your call is important. Please stay on the line. A representative will be with you shortly."

This is progress?

This is communication?

The keyboard, monitor, e-mail, fax, modem, and recording are in. The voice is out. So when we do communicate by mouth, it often comes out exactly sounding as if it's "small talk."

- "Hi."
- "How ya doin'?"
- "Nice to see you."
- "What's new?"
- "I saw Joe yesterday."
- "Right."
- "Uh-huh."

It all sounds the same as the typical greeting on an elevator first thing in the morning. I call it "the non-greeting greeting."

The lack of animation that has sneaked into "small talk" now dominates the world of spoken communication. And our role models offer little or no help. Pay attention to the way the politician or the CEO delivers a speech. The way the correspondent reads the news on television. The way the "expert" analyzes in the public forum. Or, worst of all, the way the movie star delivers lines. If you pay attention, you'll notice how little color, enthusiasm, or vividness are communicated. It all sounds exactly the same as "small talk." A keyboard kind of dullness has taken over the whole world of communication. It's not unusual that when a TV reporter says, "Three thousand people are missing in the flood," the words come out exactly as though they were, "I had a rotten cup of coffee on my way to work." Monotony reigns supreme.

A presidential radio address is a big snore.

The weatherperson speed-reads copy and may as well be reciting the phone book.

I've been at more than one meeting and heard corporate CEOs say, "We're delighted with the results this year," and it came out exactly as if they'd said, "I'm having a serious digestive problem this morning."

So why are we bothering to speak? What are we trying to say, and why can't we say it right? How can we get our audience to pay attention and take away the message we're trying to deliver? After all, if we can't do it right, why bother?

To answer these questions let's go back to the first sentence of this book, to my definition of communication. "Communication is the transfer of information from one mind to another mind, or to a group of other minds." In this age of high-tech healthcare, I call communication an information transplant. The communicator's job is to perform information surgery on the listener. The same holds true for all the other communication forms I mentioned: written, spoken, drawn, or physical (such as movement, gesture, dance, and sign language). If you have nothing to communicate, *don't*. The trick is to make the message immediately understood. The written word and the spoken word take on multiple duties. The meaning must be clear instantaneously. The feeling must be clear. The sub-text has to be clear. One advantage the written word has over the spoken word is that the eye can go back over what the mind didn't understand. When you're distracted by a hair on the page, you can reread. When you come across an unfamiliar word, you can look it up. More often than not, the spoken word gets only one chance. No one interrupts the State of the Union address and shouts, "Would you repeat that?" or, "What do you mean by that?" The same is true of most speeches.

These days good written communication is as hard to come by as good spoken communication. Many of the principles in this book that cover speech will also work for writing. But not all great writing lends itself to being spoken. Lincoln's opening words at Gettysburg ("Four score and seven years ago...") wouldn't work for today's audience. By the time we figured out he meant 87 years, he'd be into "...shall not perish from the earth." I question whether any speech other than a presidential inaugural could have gotten away with, "Ask not what your country can do for you."

To repeat, communication is about instant understanding. It's about the audience, your listeners, going away with the message you intended for them.

Too many speechwriters are writing for posterity. They hope to create great literature. They either don't know or have forgotten that the speech should be written for the speaker's conversational style and for the audience's ear.

The spoken word is what this book is about, and it can be very tricky. You can have the best message in the world, but if you don't present that message the way you intended it, you're probably communicating the wrong message. I remember my father's way of praising my mother's cooking. Somewhere mid-meal he'd look up, without expression, nod, and say in a true monotone, "'s all right." Anyone who didn't know him would have assumed he was about to throw up. Had he been forced to write his opinion on paper, he'd probably have written, "I really enjoyed the meal." On the page it's hard to misread that sentence, but spoken without enthusiasm, without inflection, without animation, it can seem to be the opposite.

Everything you do sends a signal to the audience. The way you look at me, the way you use your hands, the way you stand or sit, the inflection in your voice, all cause me to reach certain conclusions about you. This book is about the signals you send, how you send them, and how your listener receives them.

Selling Yourself

There are three things we all need in order to sell ourselves:

- Competence.
- Likability.
- Luck.

The first two will almost always deliver the third. But having competence and likability isn't enough. Most of us already have them. What's needed, and what this book will emphasize, is the audience's *perception* that you're competent and likable. It isn't about faking it, or fooling the audience. The con man and professional liar already know how to do it. They're the ones who helped the stand-up comic create the line "Sincerity: Once you learn how to fake it, you've got it made." Real people, including you and me, need to learn some basic techniques that will let us be our real selves in the presentation situation.

And therein lies the root of the problem: being ourselves.

In 1977, there was a best-seller called *The Book of Lists.* In it, there was a category titled "The Fourteen Worst Human Fears." Number one? "Speaking before a group." "Death" was six.

Fear

Lack of familiarity with the formal speaking situation, discomfort, and the thought, "They're all looking at *me* and I'm going to make a fool of myself," all conspire to cause us to take on a strange persona, to try to look and act professional. In a sense, we become actors. Bad actors, but actors.

Get Real

We make the very common mistake of feeling that an audience needs to see the strong, competent, mature professional, forgetting that that's what we really are. So we make the foolish decision to try to *impress* the audience, when the true reason for the communication is to *express* ourselves to them. Again, we're so eager to be something we think we're supposed to be that we change out of our real selves into a caricature. We become cartoon creatures.

There was a wonderful and defining moment I happened on one night, watching a television news program. The reporter was inside police headquarters. The shot showed the reporter in the foreground, speaking to the camera. Two officers were seated in the background. They were chatting behind the reporter, unaware that they were in the shot and that the tape was rolling. Their faces were animated. They were gesturing naturally. Suddenly they realized they were in the TV picture. That was it. They wiped their faces clean of all expression, put on a posed "mask," and stared straight ahead, necks taut, jaws tight, not having any idea of what to do next.

In an instant they went from being real people to mannequins. They couldn't believe that the audience should see them as anything but serious police officers. They put on an act. They simply didn't know how to be natural, to be themselves.

That's almost exactly what most of us do when we're getting ready for a picture-taking session. We chat. We converse. We have a pleasant time talking to the people around us, until suddenly the photographer says, "Look over here. Hold it!" Almost everyone immediately stiffens up. After all, this is for posterity. We have to look good. So we *change*. We simply don't know how to stay relaxed and comfortable. We don't know how to be ourselves.

The former president of the Indianapolis Chamber of Commerce wrote the following letter to me:

Dear Arch,

Recently I was on a panel reviewing a program application. The speaker gave an oral presentation then sat and answered questions. It was as if two people were making the presentation!

The first was stiff, short of breath, pacing the floor...and had a "closed face." The second was relaxed, used hand gestures, had a very "open face," and cleared up much of what was missed by the "first person."

Later, I asked if the speaker was familiar with your work. The answer was yes, and I could see the light bulb go on overhead! The lesson worked, and I was pleased I could share again how much more effective we can be when we follow your lead.

—John S. Myrland

Relax

What's important is learning to appear natural in the unnatural speaking situation. When you learn and understand what you do in animated conversation, you can convert that into the platform delivery. Unfortunately, we have very few really good role models. Most of the speakers we see and hear today are imitating what they've seen other bad presenters do. "I have to look professional in order to impress the audience," we think. Wrong. Most of the people running for public office, most of the so-called "experts" and analysts we see on television, most teachers, most speakers we watch at meetings, and certainly most of the people we watch on televised hearings, do a better job of putting us to sleep than Ambien or Lunesta.

You don't have to imitate them.

You shouldn't try to imitate them.

This is about being yourself—you at your *best*.

Be Yourself

You may not like the idea, but you might as well face the fact that style is, and always has been, at least as importance as substance, that likability is more important than competence. Teachers need to learn this. Preachers need to learn this. Trial lawyers and their witnesses need to learn this. Ordinary people in every walk of life need to learn this. You and I need to learn this to be successful.

Be Your *Likable* Self

If I perceive you to be competent, you are competent as far as I'm concerned. If I perceive you to be likable, you are. It's that simple.

Go back to the 1996 presidential election. Bill Clinton wasn't scoring high on trustworthiness, but Bob Dole didn't display a single iota of likability. He needed an intravenous feeding of charisma. Consequently, Clinton was elected. He really didn't win—Dole lost. Sure, Dole got votes, but they were the votes of Orthodox Republicans and people who despised Clinton.

Ronald Reagan won *twice*. Why? A vast majority of non-committed voters liked him. It's true and it's simple: We elect the person we like more, or dislike less.

Why the 2000 Election Was a Draw

Neither candidate had a greater likability factor than the other.

If George W. Bush had made his speeches and debate presentations the way he talked to the folks in the assisted-living facilities or the kids in fifth-grade classrooms, he'd have won hands-down. If Al Gore had delivered his presentations the way he presented his concession speech, he'd have been president.

The Private Versus the Public Image

Just about everyone I've ever trained who has been "up close and personal" with any of the recent presidential candidates insisted that they were great one-on-one or in small social groups of friends and supporters.

I heard it about Bob Dole.

I heard it about George Bush, father and son.

I heard it about Al Gore.

I heard it about John Kerry.

And then I heard it about all the too-many '08 candidates.

Each of them had no trouble being warm and enjoyable to be with. They were even accused by those who knew them of having wonderful senses of humor. But the rest of us never saw those traits. The candidates simply didn't know how to be themselves in situations they felt required them to appear "presidential" rather than friendly.

Reagan mastered the art of being himself and that let us perceive him as likable. Some people considered him to be "acting." That's nonsense. He was having a great time being governor of California and then president of the United States. He didn't have to act. He always seemed relaxed, comfortable, in control, and confident. He was so likable that he made mincemeat out of two opponents with far higher IQs than his. Higher IQs, yes, but not smart enough to know that if your message isn't delivered well, people won't care about you, and won't pay attention to your message. That was exactly what happened to Walter Mondale when he ran against Reagan. He said that Reagan was a terrific communicator, but that he, Mondale, didn't want to be remembered that way; he wanted to be remembered as the candidate of ideas. Well, no one paid any attention to his ideas other than his loyal followers.

Ironically, had I proposed coaching to Dole, Gore, George W. Bush, Hillary Clinton, Giuliani, Obama, McCain, Romney, Edwards, or anyone else you name, I'm certain he or she'd have fought me off, saying, "Look, you're not going to make an actor out of me. The person you see campaigning is the *real me.*" That's nonsense. They never talked to the public the way they talked to a spouse, family, a close friend, or a pet.

I shared a barber with George H.W. Bush. His name was Milton Pitts, and he cut Nixon's, Ford's, Reagan's, and Bush's hair. He often talked about hairstyles for television appearances during training programs I participated in at the U.S. Chamber of Commerce. Milt watched business leaders and association executives improve dramatically as communicators.

One day when I was in his chair he said to me, "Arch, George Bush is the nicest person I've ever met. He's got a great sense of humor. He's caring. If he trusts you he'll do anything in the world for you. Can you help him?"

I told Milt I felt I could help anyone who wanted to improve as a communicator. He said, "You write him a letter and give it to me with a copy of your books and the next time he's in my chair I'll hand them to him." Now, if you'd like a definition of networking, that's it!

I wrote to the vice president, saying that Milt told me he was warm, witty, and wonderful, but, unfortunately for him, I'd never seen *that* George Bush. I urged him to get professional training so that the public would see him the way Barbara, the grandkids, and Millie, the granddog, saw him.

Here's the letter I got back:

> Dear Mr. Lustberg,
>
> Milt gave me that very nice letter from you dated March 10th. I read it carefully and I also looked over the booklets. Heaven knows I could learn a lot from you. The problem is I am now working with a couple of other professionals in the field. I know that there is plenty of room for improvement in my speech making. That you were interested enough to offer to help really counts with me.
>
> Most Sincerely and Gratefully,
>
> George Bush

The Right Versus the Wrong Direction

I was really pleased to hear that he was getting help. But I watched. And I watched. And I never saw any sign of improvement. I'm convinced his coaches said, "Look, you're fighting the wimp factor. Take the gloves off," and worked on the wrong things. The reality of his warmth and caring never replaced the perception that he was angry, uptight, and uncomfortable communicating with the public.

My point was demonstrated perfectly on the Friday night after the 1996 election. Bob Dole, the defeated candidate, appeared on David Letterman's show. He took off what I call his "Leadership," or "Presidential Mask," and said these magic words with a warm glow he'd never displayed in his entire political career: "Now I can go back to being myself."

Exactly! Where was the real you during the campaign, Bob? Why did you refuse to let us see the "real" you? He never realized that the "act" he'd been putting on for us was the main reason he lost the election. He'd have given anything to win the presidency. He'd waited all his life for the chance. But he never learned how to show us the real Bob Dole, the one Elizabeth saw.

I'm convinced that if he'd had as much fun running for president as he had selling Viagra, he'd have run for reelection in 2000. Incidentally, Bob Dole named his dog Leader. Bill Clinton's dog was Buddy. That speaks volumes. As I said, his opponent was untrustworthy, but Dole was unlikable. One more time: *Likability wins.*

Presidential candidates, as are most untrained public speakers, are bad actors.

A long time ago, Dave Wilson, a client who became a close friend, said these words to me: "Public speaking is a performing art." I thought a lot about that. I was concerned that if I used that in my training, clients would hear me saying I wanted to make actors out of them. No one in the non-theater world wants acting lessons. That would be phony. Then I realized the key difference is that the actor's art is showing you someone else. The performer's art is showing you himself at his best. I learned the difference between the actor and the performer the hard way. We were three students at Catholic University's Speech and Drama Department in Washington, D.C. Two of us were World War II veterans and the other was a recent high school graduate.

Walter Kerr, who would later become the drama critic for the *New York Times,* was a faculty member and one of our teachers. He had finished an adaptation of Aristophanes' *The Birds* and was getting ready for production.

Kerr called the three of us into his office. We couldn't imagine why. He didn't mince words: "I want you three to audition for *The Birds.* There are three very special parts, and I don't want actors—I want performers."

We should have been thrilled to be wanted by a distinguished director, to be selected for our talent over all the other students. But we were devastated. Here we were, young aspiring Oliviers, being told that we weren't considered actors.

Kerr's evaluation proved to be right on the money for two of us. Ed McMahon and I went on to hone our performing skills. The third, Philip Bosco, became America's leading classical actor, interpreting the likes of Shakespeare, Moliere, and Shaw.

As it turned out, our teacher wanted three individual, unique, solo vaudeville turns, and he got them.

Here's what I subsequently discovered: Bosco, the consummate actor, was also a fine performer. McMahon and I were fine performers who couldn't act.

So, to return to an earlier thought, the difference is that the good actor shows you—and you believe you're seeing—someone else. The good performer shows you himself at his best.

All spoken communication should be you presenting the real you; your warmest, most pleasant self. That's what the likability factor is all about.

The Power of Perception

Obviously, I'm talking about the power of perception. Some years ago you were watching an entertainment show on television. The show cut away to a commercial. Then a 10-second promo came on for the late news. Then back to another commercial. The news teaser you saw was a close-up of the anchorperson saying, "Superstar Michael Jackson is under investigation today by the Los Angeles Police for sexually molesting a 13-year-old boy. At 10."

So at 10 p.m. we turned on the news and it opened exactly the same way: The anchor, looking stern, severe, and sincere, said the same words, "Superstar Michael Jackson is under investigation today for sexually molesting a 13-year-old boy." Then the picture cut away. The anchor was gone. but we heard the same voice saying, "sleeping with...fondling...touching the private parts of...." It was a whole laundry list of suggestive sex words. And do you remember what they showed you? There, on the screen, bigger than life, was Michael Jackson doing the "Moonwalk," tugging at his crotch, and massaging his privates as he strutted back and forth across the stage. Guilty!

After that you saw the same video footage over and over again. It was repeated as often as the Rodney King beating, the O.J. Bronco chase, and Bill Clinton hugging Monica Lewinsky. Sure, it's overkill, but it helps reinforce a specific perception. And that perception may not be reality.

So, if I perceive you to be incompetent, you're incompetent. At least, that's what you are to me. If I perceive you to be unlikable, you *are.* The fact that you're really competent and likable doesn't mean a thing. Unfortunately, very few people have learned the secrets of communicating competence and likability.

Communicating Competence and Likability

Selling yourself is just that. It's the ability to let the audience—the person or people you're talking to—see you as competent and likable. Again, if they don't like you and find you less than competent, you haven't got a chance. If they see you as competent and likable, your message gets across.

When the candidate you don't like and don't consider capable tells you he'll cut your taxes and give you more and better services, you think he's either a liar or an ass. When the same pledge comes from the candidate you really like, who impresses you as knowledgeable, you're ready to elect him emperor, new clothes or otherwise.

We can learn a lot from watching our politicians.

Issues and ideas are meaningless to an audience until and unless they're presented in a likable, believable way. My hope is that someday we'll have two likable candidates running for the same office. Only then will we be able to cut through the garbage and get the message they want us to hear.

How the Public Views You

One more concept I should emphasize here: There are three points of view possible in any audience:

- They can agree with you.
- They can disagree with you.
- They can be undecided.

Your job as a communicator is to reach out and win the undecided.

When the political candidate understands this fact, winning is easier. When the trial lawyer gets it, the case is presented with a better chance to convince the jury. When the salesman becomes aware of it, the sale has a better chance of closure.

Aim for the Undecided

Don't waste your time with the people on your side. They're already yours. I'm not telling you to ignore them. I'm just saying you're wasting your time concentrating on them. They're already committed unless you blunder badly. You're preaching to the choir.

Forget about trying to convince the people on the other side. You're not likely to make a convert with a good presentation. They're already convinced that you're wrong, or a crackpot, or worse.

The only people who matter are the folks who haven't made up their minds: the undecided. And how do you win them? By presenting yourself as a competent and likable person.

Here's what I tell my political candidate clients: I can't guarantee that my training will get you elected. But I can guarantee that if you use my principles of likability, you'll get more votes than you'd have gotten without them.

Selling Your Competence

There are four communication tools available to each of us:

- Your mind.
- Your face.
- Your body.
- Your voice.

I'm going to oversimplify matters by calling the way you use your mind the audience's determination of your competence; and your face, body, and voice your likability. We can call your mind your "substance." Your face, body, and voice your "style." Or we can refer to your mind as "what you say," and the other three as "how you say it."

I realize that it's an oversimplification. There are large areas of overlap, but it really helps me simplify and synthesize my points for you.

Your Competence

Let's start with the audience's perception of your competence. Your competence is reflected in the way you use your mind. It's how you organize your thoughts. It's how you use that great personal computer called your brain and how you get it to bring the right message up on its screen. Too often the screen tells you "bad command." By that time it's too late.

What Can You Do?

You need to help the audience realize that you're a competent, capable person.

Prepare

Very few people are wonderful when they're winging it. Some are naturals, but most are not. It usually takes a lot of hard work to appear spontaneous. Mark Twain wrote, "It usually takes me three weeks to prepare a good impromptu speech." The old vaudeville rule is, "It takes a lot of hard work to appear to be ad-libbing."

Your Strengths

Never forget that you know more than anyone else about certain things. You grew up in a particular family, attended specific schools and churches, had certain friends and influences on your life, and had your own jobs.

You are unique. Use this to your advantage.

Only you can put it all together in your particular way. But do it with care. Even the most sophisticated computer needs an instant—a split second—to respond. So the most important step in responding to a question or an accusation is to let your preparation work for you, and the way to do that is to *pause*.

The Audible Pause

The pause is the key to the fine art of thinking on your feet. We don't like to pause. We think, "If I take too long to reply, they're going to think I'm stupid."

This is why the pause has become unnatural. We either plunge ahead from thought to thought, stopping only long enough to suck in a sufficient supply of air to spit out the next fact (the way the weatherperson on TV does), or we fill our pauses with competence-defeating sounds. "I...uh... think...uh...we should...uh...act on the...uh...assumption...uh...that we're all...uh...uh...adults."

By the time that sentence is finished, you not only question the competence of the speaker, but you wish you were somewhere else.

Our role models are no help either. People who've reached high positions deluge us with "...uh...um...er." It's not unusual to be settling in on an airplane and suddenly hear over the loudspeaker, "Uh... folks...uh...this is your...uh...captain...uh...speaking. We're...uh...currently climbing through...uh...12,000 feet...uh...up to our...uh...cruising altitude of...uh...33,000...uh...(and by now you're ready to scream, "Feet, Captain, feet!"). You just hope the pilot isn't as tentative at the controls.

Don't Imitate Bad Examples

It happened a long time ago, but it's worth bringing back here. It was July 31, 1987. My assistant called and said, "Turn your tape recorder on. Secretary of Defense Casper Weinberger is stumbling through congressional testimony." The subject was continuing aid to the Contras.

Here's what the tape played back:

> *I think it's even more vital now that...uh...all of this...uh... uh...all of these...uh...uh...attempts...or...whatever...it... were...that...were...made...uh...to...uh...assist...in...uh...uh... uh...non...uh...uh...mmmuh...straightforward and...uh... and...uh...means that are provided for in our regular statutory...uh...uh...framework—that none of that distract us from the basic importance and...and...essential correctness of the...uh...of the requirement of...of...supporting the...uh...the...uh...democratic resistance in Nicaragua.*

Try to figure out that statement. I dare you.

Even professionals can blunder

You may not have noticed it, but even television reporters fall into the trap. They're used to reading from TelePrompTers as their scripts roll between their eyes and the camera lens. But on those occasions when breaking news forces them to "wing it," notice how flustered they become.

It's not unusual to hear, "The...uh...fire is...uh...reported to...uh...have broken out at...uh...just after...uh...midnight."

They Ought to Know Better, *But!*

The athlete, the jock, has given us two words that never existed before $16 zillion salaries for mediocre shortstops: "ya know." There isn't a sportscast that doesn't have: "Ya know, George, ya know, we went out on strike, ya know, because the owners, ya know, they were, ya know, unreasonable, ya know."

I know.

Soon after she was elected to the U.S. Senate, Hillary Clinton held a news conference. Asked about her husband's presidential pardons, she said "you know" 19 times—three times in one sentence. There were also plenty of "uhs." And during the 2008 campaign, the word *like* reared its ugly head.

On CNN, reporting the "breaking news," anchor Lou Waters said, "She...uh...demonstrated complete...uh...control and...uh...cool throughout the...uh...presentation."

Beware of Useless Catchwords and Phrases

Teenagers add "and so," "know what I mean?" and "okay?"

Most of us overuse "I think," "I believe," "as a matter of fact," "to be perfectly honest," "frankly," "if I may say so," "as it were," and "if I may."

This is pure garbage.

Many wise men of the past have said the same thing in different ways. Euripides wrote, "Second thoughts are ever wiser." Dionysius the Elder said, "Let thy speech be better than silence, or be silent." Pericles is quoted: "The man who can think and does not know how to express what he thinks is at the level of him who cannot think."

Make the Pause Work for You

Use the silent pause and *really* think on your feet.

We've developed a disease that I call intellectual dysentery. Sounds keep pouring out of our mouths uncontrollably. When the people who do it hold a position of responsibility, we have no choice but to question their competence. And the worst scenario is when the audience knows the next word before the speaker is able to...uh...get it...uh...uh...out.

Become Aware

It's not enough to know about the "audible pause." You need to become aware of it as you do it. My suggestion is that you ask someone you trust, like, and are comfortable with to send you a small signal each time you do it in conversation—something such as a small, inconspicuous head nod.

After you've seen the signal a couple of times, you'll start to hear yourself as you do it. And until you become aware of it, you won't be able to control it. Now, as you hear it...uh...(there, I heard that), you'll be able to control it the next time, and, pretty soon, it's gone 50 percent of the time. No one minds an occasional intrusive sound. It's only when it happens during almost every pause that it becomes a competence defeater.

Step one in protecting competence is to pause silently.

Step two is to maintain steady, warm, non-intimidating eye contact. It's as important a demonstrator of competence as the silent pause. And it's just as unnatural.

Eye Contact

This is a terribly misunderstood concept because we all interpret it to mean eye to eye, and that's often a mistake.

All our lives we remember being told to "look 'em in the eye." But many people find that very uncomfortable and stressful, especially at close range. Eye-to-eye contact is often a challenge, an invitation to compete, a contest to see who blinks first. In fact, it's such an uncomfortable encounter for some people that they think better when looking away from the person they're talking to.

Certainly, if looking into someone else's eyes for an extended time doesn't bother you, then eye to eye is fine.

Where to Look

In a television interview a few years before he died, James Stewart credited Marlene Dietrich with teaching him where to look. She told him that when two people looked into each other's eyes, they kept shifting from one eye to the other eye. The result: They looked "shifty-eyed." And, of course, in a close camera shot, the movement was magnified.

Still worse, when two people are staring into each other's eyes, their concentration is easily broken as they get into the staring match. Miss Dietrich also suggested to Mr. Stewart that most actors tend to break up in unexplainable laughter when the contact is eye to eye. She recommended a place in the center of the head: the brow, the nose, or the mouth.

Sir Laurence Olivier often yelled at actors working with him, "Stop looking in my eyes!" It broke his concentration.

Select Your Own Spot

I like to look at the mouth. I'm a lip reader. I believe I hear you better if I watch you form your words. So I'll look at your mouth, unless you're missing two front teeth. In that case, I'll switch to your brow, unless there's an enormous zit up there. Then I'll move to your nose, unless there's a strange object dangling from one of your nostrils.

What I'm suggesting is that, if eye-to-eye contact is stressful or intimidating or uncomfortable for you, find a place on the face of the person you're talking to, and stay there. The important point to remember here is that the people you're talking to are unaware that you're not looking them in the eye. Eye contact means to look *at* someone. It doesn't mean to make someone uncomfortable by "staring 'em down."

Avoid Bad Role Models

Again, we're victims of our role models in this matter.

Very few people find it comfortable to maintain steady eye contact.

So we glance down. Maybe the floor will help us think.

Or we look up. "Please, Lord, help me out of this situation."

Or we look side-to-side. "I am not a crook."

Notice the way attorneys are portrayed in scenes by actors who've researched courtroom behavior. The actor paces and prances before the jury, arms gesticulating, voice filled with fire and brimstone, eyes glued to the floor in front of him as he paces, looking for all the world as the attorney trained in law school to hunt for roaches.

I'm sure you've been at a reception where the person you're talking to glances away regularly. It may not be his intention, but it looks as though he's checking to see if someone more important has come into the room.

Practice With a Friend

Try the following exercise with a friend.

- Introduce yourself looking away as your friend looks at you.
- Now look at your friend.
- Have your friend look away as you introduce yourself.
- Now look at each other as you introduce yourself.
- Now reverse roles with your friend as introducer in the three scenarios.

It's a perfect example. When eye contact is called for and not used, no communication is possible. In fact, it's almost laughable.

Remember: Each of you sees the other's eyes in your peripheral vision. I've asked literally hundreds of people if they could tell where I was looking. Nearly everyone thought I was making eye-to-eye contact.

Without the combination of silence and eye contact in the pause, you're inflicting major damage on yourself. An audience will find it very hard, if not impossible, to perceive you as a competent person.

Preparation

You're also going to be judged on the basis of what you say, on your information. Here again, this is about *preparation*, not about what to say. That's your strong suit. You know your subject.

This is about how to put it together and how to say it.

How to Say It

My focus is on *how* to say it. It would be presumptuous of outsiders to tell you *what* to say.

That being said, there are a few thoughts worth mentioning here. You really don't need me to tell you that most speakers take far too long to say what they have to say. I'm sure you're aware of that already.

Even in conversation, it isn't unusual for people to say too much. Most speeches, presentations, and meetings go on beyond human endurance.

Lou Cook, former president of the Alexandria, Virginia, school board, uses this adage: "Sometimes the mind can absorb only what the seat can endure."

When he was CEO of Continental Airlines, Gordon Bethune did an interview with Merrill Lynch's *Advisor* magazine. He was asked about the collapse of the airlines, and said, "The fuel gauge didn't work, the hydraulic system was broken, and we were flying upside-down." Then he was asked why he was still insisting on providing food on longer flights when all the others were cutting it out, he said, "I didn't think it was the right time to take the cheese off the pizza."

Practice economy.

First

Start by telling them what they want to know.

I'm not saying tell them what they want to hear.

That's the classic mistake of the political consultant who guides elected officials with gimmickry and poll numbers.

Second

If there's still interest, add what you feel they *need* to know.

Third

When you're finished, *stop*.

...

That is the hardest job of all for the professional windbag. And nobody likes a windbag. Not even another windbag.

What They Want to Know

This is the information you can share with them that affects them personally.

The key question to ask yourself is, "What does this have to do with their lives?" In other words, "How is this information relevant to the people in my audience?"

If you relate your message to their family, their pocketbook, their job security, their social security, healthcare, and other benefits, their children's and grandchildren's well-being, you can sell them on your ideas. They're hooked.

Your material can be presented factually, anecdotally, or pictorially, but it has to involve the audience by way of the story you tell and the presentation of that story.

People I train are constantly telling me, "But Arch, my material is dull." I have news for them and for you: There's no such thing as dull material. Only dull presenters.

Early in the first Clinton administration, the big issue was healthcare. The president and first lady started off brilliantly. They were terrific with statements such as, "If your mother is in a nursing home, it's probably costing you upwards of $3,500 a month to keep her there. When you run out of money, your mother runs out of care. That's not fair!"

Or, "A woman in Detroit just had her dialysis machine removed from her home. She can't afford the payments. That means you and I have sentenced that woman to die!"

There were lots of other truthful, dramatic stories that really got us to pay attention. They were selling their plan.

More Than They Want to Know

Then they made the mistake of trying to explain all the minute details of a healthcare plan that looked to be a book the size of the federal budget or an IRS tax code.

We simply lost interest.

And while this was putting us into a coma with anesthetics such as, "Forty percent of the population of the six largest cities will only qualify for 8 percent of the reimbursed funds in 16 percent of the for-profit healthcare institutions providing equivalent quality of patient care...zzzzzzzzz," on came Harry and Louise in TV commercials sponsored by anti-Clinton healthcare forces.

Harry: Louise, if their rotten healthcare scheme goes through, you won't be able to see Dr. Gordon!

Louise: I won't???

H: No. They're going to force you to see some other doctor, one they pick for you.

L: But I've been with Dr. Gordon for 15 years.

H: Well, they're not going to let you see him.

L: But he already knows everything about my condition.

H: That doesn't matter to them. They want to be big brother. They think they know better what's good for you.

L: How can they do that?

H: It's a big, bureaucratic boondoggle. It's a lousy healthcare scheme and we have to fight for our rights. The little guy just doesn't count any more.

Each side began with what we wanted to know, but one side got long-winded, droned on and on, and dropped the ball. It was no contest.

And failing in that contest became a point of contention for Hillary in the '08 campaign.

What They Need to Know

The perfect example of this concept was the prosecution's case presenting the DNA evidence in the O.J. Simpson criminal trial. I believe the prosecutors spent more than two weeks on DNA matters. It seemed interminable.

When the trial began, most Americans had no idea what the letters "DNA" stood for. In fact, we still don't know what the letters spell out. As the trial progressed, the presentation of the DNA evidence was endless.

The jury's eyes glazed over.

The testimony became meaningless.

There was simply nothing to hold on to.

Then, of course, the defense took advantage of the impossibly dull DNA testimony of experts and called on lots more of them to take the jurors off life support.

Short, quick, and to the point

What about this approach:

A chart depicting three distinct DNA symbols marked "A," "B," and "C" is placed in the front of the courtroom.

Prosecutor: Dr. Brooks, are you considered an expert on DNA evidence?

Doctor: Yes.

P: Is there a simple way to describe what DNA is?

D: It's like a genetic identification bracelet.

P: Doctor, is it accepted as accurate identification in criminal trials and accepted as admissible evidence?

D: It has been in trials I've participated in as a witness.

P: Doctor, looking at the chart here, is figure "A" the defendant's DNA symbol?

D: Yes.

P: Is "B" the symbol of the murdered woman?

D: Yes.

P: Is "C" the symbol identifying the murdered man?

D: Yes.

P: Doctor, is it likely that a DNA symbol of anyone in this room would exactly match any of these three?

D: No.

P: Is it likely that the DNA symbol of anyone in this country would match exactly with any of these three?

D: No.

P: Doctor, would you call the DNA as accurate an identification as a handwriting sample?

D: More accurate.

P: And, Doctor, would you call it as accurate an identification as a fingerprint?

D: More accurate.

P: Doctor, if I told you there were samples of this DNA (points to "A") on the body of the murdered woman, on the body of the murdered man, on the defendant's clothing, on his driveway, in his Bronco, and inside his house, would you say that we have the equivalent of an eyewitness to two murders?

D: Yes.

P: No further questions.

•••

What they *need* to know

That's all the jury needed to know.

Yes, the defense will object.

They'll cross-examine.

They'll put their own DNA expert witnesses on the stand.

I'm not saying that this line of questioning would have changed the outcome of the trial, but it would have been more effective than two weeks of agonizing detail and would have made it harder for the jury to acquit.

The jury needed to know the DNA evidence. It was the critical part of the trial. But the prosecution made the mistake of thinking those 12 people needed to know lots more than they really did. DNA evidence became overkill, which reinforces this final point:

*When you're finished, **stop**.*

Selling Your Likability

You give your audience four choices:

- They can like you.
- They can dislike you.
- They can be neutral to you and not care one way or the other.
- They can feel sorry for you.

The Goal

Your one goal as a communicator is to get them to like you. If the uncommitted people in your audience like you, chances are they'll pay attention and get your message. If they don't like you, they'll probably consider you pushy, or incompetent, or misguided, or bombastic, or phony. If they're neutral to you, they'll think they'd be better off spending their time somewhere else. The message won't make it across the distance between you. If they feel sorry for you, that's the message: "Poor, poor soul!" Nothing else will be communicated.

Think about this: If they like you, even if they strongly disagree with your message, the worst they can say about you is, "That one really believes that garbage," or, "So what? I like him." That was the prevailing feeling about Bill Clinton's untruths. And believe me, that's better than, "What a liar," or, "How stupid can you get?" or, "Kill!"

A Few Corollaries Already Suggested

- We never buy from a seller we don't like.

- Jurors almost never convict a defendant they really like or one whose attorney presents the client as wronged by the system. The case almost always results in an acquittal or, at worst, a hung jury.

- We rarely become close friends with people we genuinely dislike.

- We hardly ever hire the job applicant we don't like.

- We certainly don't promote the unlikable one.

- We learn better in the classroom of the teacher we like and who appears to like us. This is true even when that teacher is a strict disciplinarian.

- We never vote for the candidate we dislike most. In fact, even when we think the more unlikable one would do a better job, chances are we'll not even go to the polling place this time.

- We all know people we don't care for. We go out of our way not to socialize with them. We think, "We have nothing in common."

- We all have family members we don't like, and the only reason we put up with them is just that: They're family.

- We all have colleagues at work with varying degrees of likability. Which ones do we gravitate to at break time?

Another inescapable fact: I may like someone you don't like, and vice versa. So the logical conclusion is that there's no such thing as being liked by everyone. But the objective is to communicate in such a way that most of your audience will find you likable.

Keys to Likability

Your use of face, body, and voice are your keys to likability. Obviously, we're all using them constantly to communicate. But most of us are using them incorrectly.

Using Your Face

The first thing the audience sees is your face. It's hard to realize, but that first look is going to cause the audience to make a judgment about you. It's an instantaneous feeling of like, dislike, neutrality, or pity. We never realize it, but our "public" face is quite different from our "personal" or "social" face.

Make it a point to begin watching other people in all kinds of common situations, such as getting on an elevator, nodding a greeting at someone in the office first thing in the morning, getting on a bus or subway, or at the checkout counter. There's almost never an expression of genuine warmth, caring, or affection.

That brings me to my third definition of communication.

Remember:

1. Communication is the transfer of information from mind to mind.

2. Communication is an information transplant.

3. Communication is an intellectual act of love.

It's a heavy concept. It takes a lot of thought to accept. But it happens to be true. An audience reacts in kind. When you look as though you're ill at ease as you speak, you make your audience feel the same way about you. When you look as though you don't care about your audience, they don't care back. But when you make intellectual love to your audience, they have no choice but to like you back.

And never forget: *Likability wins.*

The smile

First, consider the smile. It says, "I'm happy to be here." It's a wonderful way to introduce yourself. It's a wonderful recurring tool for any communicator. But a word of caution: In order to be effective, the smile has to be two things. It has to be genuine, and it has to be absolutely appropriate. Otherwise, you'll resemble the village idiot. Picture the person smiling and saying, "I'm sorry about the death in your family," or, "Let's talk now about AIDS."

It always comes as a shock when the TV reporters look as if they're smiling or grinning when they broadcast, "Three thousand people were left homeless when the earthquake struck in Nepal," or the weather reporter who appears to be having a great time telling you, "Another tornado is on the way in the Southeast."

The smiling face is a happy face. It must only appear at happy or pleasant times. Many women have said to me, "People tell me I smile too much." My answer to them is, "Maybe the smile appears too often at inappropriate times." I don't think it's possible to smile too much if the message is a pleasant, happy one. A famous former National Football League quarterback has a jaw formation that makes him look as if he's grinning when he's not. He has a huge mouth, enormous teeth, and lips that have never met. He'd throw a pass, and it would be intercepted and returned for a touchdown by the other team. He'd pull off his helmet and leave the field with what appeared to be a huge smile. Believe me, he wasn't smiling, but the look once caused John Madden to comment, "What's he so happy about?" Of course, I'm talking about John Elway.

There is such a thing as a nervous smile. It's an unfortunate face to show. I'm thinking of the person who's being interviewed on television at a moment of terrible stress. Quite often you'll see the grieving widow talking about the accident that took her husband's life telling the interviewer what a terrible experience it was, and the near-grimace comes across as a grin. We wonder if he had a fabulous insurance policy. Or the people you've seen talking to a reporter while cleaning up after a devastating flood. The face is really in a resigned "acceptance" mode, but again, it appears as a grin, and we're left wondering.

Non-smiling faces

There are three non-smiling faces we're capable of showing to others. I call them the "closed face," the "neutral face," and the "open face." Each is produced by the use of the involuntary muscles of the face. By that I mean we use them all the time without realizing what we're doing.

The closed face. This is the name I give to the face we produce when we frown. We draw the brows tightly together (it's called the "knit" brow). We narrow the eye slits. (And remember: The eyes are the window to the soul.) And we produce a vertical line or lines between the eyebrows.

Closed face: The closed face is perceived as an angry face. It's a sure loser.

We do it all the time when we're deep in thought. ("That's a tough one. Let me think about it for a minute.") This is the face we use all the time when we're worried. ("Doctor, tell me the truth. Is it cancer? Am I going to die?") And we do it when we're angry. ("You promised me a raise. You lied!") It's a terrible face to show an audience. It almost always comes across as stressed out, furious, or sneaky, and an audience simply doesn't like what it sees. You look as though you don't like your audience, and your audience dislikes you back. For example, the closed face almost defeated George W. Bush twice.

The neutral face. This is the name I give to the face you show when nothing moves but the mouth.

Neutral face: The neutral face is a bored, uncaring face. It's another loser.

It's the most common public-speaking and television-interviewee face. The face is naked. We don't want the audience to see us naked, so we "put it away." We hide it. We put on a mask. It's the face of "small talk." Unfortunately, it's the face we use most of the time. It's the face of the dead.

Pay attention to the speakers at the next meeting you attend.

Watch experts giving their wisest opinion on TV.

Watch political candidates.

Again, look at other people on the elevator and on public transportation. They look as if the casket business should be booming.

The neutral face seems to be saying, "I don't care one whit about you," and the audience reciprocates in kind. It's the surest way to turn off the listeners' attention buttons. For example, the neutral face cost Al Gore a victory in the 2000 election, and cost John Kerry in 2004. I felt that the neutral face was the reason it was so hard to predict the outcome of the 2008 primaries. In an effort to resemble a genuine commander-in-chief, every candidate made the Bob Dole "leader" mistake and failed to show you a warm, caring human being. Throughout the entire '08 campaign, I said that the real shame was that Elizabeth Edwards wasn't running. She embodied the essence of likability. Nothing phony, just a real person.

The open face. Now comes the element of my training I'm proudest of. It's the expression I call the open face. I created the concept when I started teaching in 1952. It's a winner. It's the face that says, "I like you." It's a caring face.

People who've been through my training agree that it's the most useful, most helpful concept they've ever learned. They've discovered, and I hope you'll discover, that when you make intellectual love to your audience, they have no choice but to really like you back.

Nearly every follow-up of my training for Merrill Lynch financial consultants talks about the life-changing and career-improving effect of the open face.

I treasure this letter from a woman I never met:

Dear Mr. Lustberg,

I am writing to thank you. You have made quite an impact on my husband. He sat next to you on an airplane a couple of weeks ago. The two of you had a conversation about communicating effectively, and the impact that facial expressions have on other people. He demonstrated the "open" face for everyone he met and explained why it was preferable to a "closed" face.

He is a consultant for a large corporation and travels extensively. Every few months he finds himself in a new assignment with a whole new group of co-workers. This is challenging and intimidating for him. He is not known for a "gets along with everyone" personality. He considers himself quite intelligent and tends to come across a little arrogant at times.

On the trip from the airport to his new assignment, a corporate colleague informed him that one of the other employees at the work site was a little difficult to deal with. He was advised to "just try to ignore her bad personality." However, he decided to take your advice to heart.

After one week of polite conversation and conscious attempts to keep an open face, this person has warmed up to him nicely. She treats him kindlier and with much greater respect than the other corporate people. His co-workers are amazed. This has boosted his confidence, eased his transition, and makes him more valuable to the project.

Thank you for taking the time to share your knowledge and insight with him. He feels as though he has a new and effective tool to help him as he meets and interacts with people.

C.L.

Open face: *The open face is a caring face, and the audience returns the favor. Remember: The smiling face is happy. The open face is warm.*

It works. So when people tell me, "I don't care if the audience likes me; that doesn't matter to me," all I can say is, "You're making a world-class mistake."

The *open face* is the face you show your audience when you elevate your brows slightly and create the horizontal lines in your forehead.

It's the face of warm, caring, animated conversation. Watch people telling secrets.

Watch two people engaged in big-time gossip.

No one has ever walked up to a baby's crib and neutrally or frowningly said, "Good morning, baby. I have a bottle. I want you to drink it. It will nourish you."

What do we do? We open up, raise our brows, and say, "Hi, baby." We show the baby the only signals of affection he or she can understand. The same is true of our relationship with our pets. We give them all the love and affection they need, but we hold back with adults for fear of looking foolish.

Again, the eyes are the window to the soul. And when you're willing to "show me more eye," I believe you're telling me the truth.

Don't be confused. Don't confuse the smile with the open face. The smile is a happy face. The open face is a caring face.

Your strongest tools

The use of the open face and eye contact are two of the strongest tools anyone can use to convince someone else. To be liked. To win. They represent the most powerful attributes of the best teachers, preachers, salespeople, witnesses, attorneys, candidates for public office, and public speakers. Even the doctors I train find that this technique dramatically improves patient relationships. And, heaven knows, bedside manner becomes more important with each passing day of managed care.

Practice

1. Try using your mirror. *Frown* at yourself and count to five aloud. See how menacing and awful you appear to an audience when you close your face.

2. Now *neutralize* your face. Don't move anything but your lips, and don't move them very much. Count to five aloud again and see how easy it will be to put an audience to sleep or make them wish they were somewhere else.

3. Next *open* your face. Move your brows up. Count aloud to five again. Notice the change. It really doesn't take a lot of exaggeration but, because we're not used to making these muscles work that way, it may seem strange at first. People often feel "bug-eyed" trying to make it happen. But after a while, practicing this exercise will help it become a much more natural expression in the unnatural circumstance of speaking in public.

When in doubt, remember the baby, the puppy, and the kitten.

Practice with a friend

In the last chapter, I suggested an eye-contact exercise with a friend. Now try it as a face exercise. Close your face. Frown hard. Now introduce yourself. Next, neutralize your face. Wipe off all the expression. Introduce yourself again. Open your face. Let your eyes open all the way and arch the brows upward. Introduce yourself. Now, have your friend do the same exercise as you watch. The difference is remarkable.

The key to likability is the open face. And remember: *Likability wins.*

Using Your Body

The second likability tool is your body. It's another key part of that critical first opinion of you. It involves the way you stand and the way you sit, your posture, and the way you use your hands and arms. I call the gesture "the communicator's equivalent of a hug or a handshake."

The gesture is like a handshake or a hug.

If you'll agree that communication is an intellectual act of love, you'll realize that the open face says, "I care," and the gesture says, "I share." So just as the face is naked, so too are the hands. We're not at all comfortable with them, so we hide them. We put them away. Standing, we immediately go into one of four "no-no" hand positions, each effectively killing any chance to use gesture as a communication tool.

The 4 "no-no" hand positions

1. One hand clutches the other wrist and together they come to rest in front of the crotch. In photography, this is called the "fig leaf" position.

   Most men and many women consider this the hand position of choice. It's almost guaranteed that as soon as the photographer bellows, *"Hold it,"* that's where we go. Most still photos we see of people standing at official gatherings feature

Fig leaf: *This position is named "the fig leaf" by photographers.*

Pockets: *You've heard the keys and change as the fingers gesture in the pockets.*

the fig leaf. Ironically, because we're all natural gesturers, we wind up flicking fingers to make a point. More overt gesturers open and close their palms in quick succession and look as though they're "flashing."

2. Hands thrust deep into pockets. Unfortunately, this gesturer is flicking hidden fingers. We've all heard the keys and the change being flung around, and it becomes a joke.

3. Hands behind the back. It's the hallmark of royalty and military leaders, people never accused of having hugging personalities.

4. The female fig leaf. Arms folded defiantly in front of the chest. Most women and many men favor this position.

All four happen to be extremely comfortable positions for us. Unfortunately, what's comfortable to us can look terribly uncomfortable and uptight to an audience.

At ease: The military mistakenly calls this position "at ease." It looks anything but.

Female fig leaf: Nothing looks more aloof and defensive than your arms folded tightly in front of you.

They are gesture-inhibiting positions.

They are hand-hiders.

They are easy, but they are wrong!

The people looking at the no-no position are made uncomfortable because the presenter appears unhappy to be in front of a group or a camera.

What's a person to do?

Once again, use your mirror. Stand erect. Shake out your shoulders. See where your hands fall. As uncomfortable as this position seems to be, it happens to be the perfect and natural starting position.

Now notice I said "starting." After the first gesture, the hands can go anywhere you're comfortable with as long as that first gesture says "keep gesturing." As the smile is, the gesture has to be appropriate and genuine. If it is, it will help you look like you mean what you say and you're saying what you mean.

When the CEO says, "The company had a wonderful year," the word *wonderful* has to be accompanied by a physical movement. Otherwise, the word might as well have been *so-so*. It's the same with the smile: The only time the gesture seems wrong is when it's not genuine or appropriate.

In conversation, most of us are constantly gesturing. How often have you heard, "If I didn't use my hands, I couldn't talk"? The gesture is a natural communication tool in our culture. Don't throw it away because you're uncomfortable with your hands.

Nothing will turn the audience to looking out the window and daydreaming as the combination of the neutral face and the fig leaf will.

Using Your Voice

Speech is an acquired habit. No one spoke at birth. We develop our speech machine primarily by imitation. That's why the Bostonian paaks his kaa, the Alabaman comes from the Sayuth, the Midwesterner goes fisheen and hunteen, the New Yorker lives in Nyawk and the Baltimorean in Ballimer, and the Kentucky Derby is run in Lawvl.

The voice is a musical instrument. Most people have forgotten that—if, in fact, they ever knew it. A spoken sentence can be likened to a line from a song: The words are the lyrics and the way the words are delivered is the music.

In fact, when speech is at its best, its most exciting, it can be traced on a musical scale.

The spoken word is guided by the face. Normally, the voice is not a signal-sender on its own. The face tells the voice what notes to hit. When the face is neutral, the voice is a dull monotone. When the face is closed, the voice is cold. When the face is open, the voice is at its best.

Try this:

- **Close your face.** Frown hard. Draw your brows tightly to-gether. Narrow those eye slits until your eyes are barely open. Now say the words: "Good morning." Hold the position and say it again. "Good morning." It sounds as though your say-ing, "I hope you're having as bad a day as I am." That's your face telling your voice what to do.

Saying "good morning" with a closed face sounds like "I'm having a rotten day. Keep your distance."

- **Neutralize your face.** Don't energize any of the facial muscles. Don't move anything but your lips and say it again. "Good morning." Nothing. No one can believe you're doing anything but forcing yourself to say two words. You might as well just nod your head or grunt a sound.

The neutral face "good morning" says, "Go away. I have more important things to do than talk to you."

- **Open your face.** Get those brows way up. Let the eyes widen and glow. Now say it. "Good morning." Listen to the music. What a change. This not only brightens the day of the person you're greeting, but it has a golden effect on your own well-being. You make other people feel better, and you feel better as well.

The open face "good morning" says, "I'm glad to see you."

It's personality therapy!

You went from angry-sounding to boring to enthusiastic, energetic, and happy. We go out of our way to show the open face to the child and the pet, but we're ashamed to use it with adults. The voice takes on its warmest tone when the open face is the signal-sender.

Do the three "good mornings" again, this time paying close attention to the signals your voice is sending.

Closed: "Good morning." Seems to say, "Get out of here. Go away."

Neutral: "Good morning." Sounds as if you're saying, "I wish I were somewhere else."

Open: "Good ^{mor} $_{ning.}$" Seems to say, "Welcome to a wonderful world."

I've always considered it remarkable that voice is taught as a separate course in high school and college. I can understand separating voice as part of a drama or music curriculum, but otherwise voice has no business being separated from the mind, the face, and the body. In other words, voice should never be taught in a vacuum. Certainly, if you have vocal problems and tend to strain your throat after speaking for a while, or if your voice is harsh, strident, shrill, nasal, or whiney, then you should get help in the production of sound. But barring a real problem, your voice will respond as it should and be pleasant to hear if your face and body are open as you speak.

Vocal tools

There are three vocal tools that you should be aware of as you speak. They are:

- **Volume** is the decibel level: the loudness or softness of your voice.

- **Pitch** is the position of the sound on the musical scale: the highness or lowness of your voice.

- **Rate** is the duration of the sound: the length of time it takes you to make it.

When we are stressed, the muscles of the head and neck tighten, and most sounds tend to come out the same. That is, every sound seems to take on the same volume, pitch, and rate, which is the definition of monotonous. When your facial muscles are tight and you say, "He made an amazing recovery," every syllable sounds exactly the same as every other syllable. You're inviting anyone listening to tune you out or to misunderstand you. When you open your face (and by that very action you're de-stressing the muscles), chances are the words will come out this way:

He made an a maaz ing recovery.

There's variety in volume, pitch, and rate inside that sentence. There's honesty in that sentence.

Volume is the most overused and the least effective of the three vocal tools.

Years ago, before refined sound systems, powerful, sonorous voices were the norm, because the speaker had to reach the back of large auditoriums. The only aid was the speaker's own vocal power. But as the technical equipment improved, the ability (or lack of ability) of most speakers remained in the 1920s. The advent of the microphone should have altered speaking styles drastically, but it hasn't. Before the microphone, it was never possible to speak in an entirely conversational voice and be heard by a large number of people. Now it is. But most inexperienced, uncomfortable, or untrained speakers tend to speak too loudly in public situations. The untrained will approach the microphone, clear the throat (which may or may not need clearing), place the voice too far back in the throat (to impress the audience with authority), and speak too loudly. The sound that comes out is pompous. It's the sound of the great "ahem," a phony voice, an affected voice, a "platform voice." Yet, many of us still do it, thinking it's the proper public voice for the serious professional. Pay attention to the politician making a speech in a large auditorium. Invariably you'll hear the volume go up.

Young men and women moving up in the world must be especially aware of this trap. It's very easy to fall into because we've been led to believe that it's what's expected in the upwardly mobile world. It isn't, but, after all, our role models, the business and political leaders we see all the time, show us very few examples of good communication skills.

One young man, seeing a television replay of his before and after presentations in a workshop said, "Now I know what you mean. You're telling me to use my 'living room' voice all the time—not my 'radio' voice." That's it exactly! You should use your warm, conversational, "living room" voice, not your "professional," "authoritative," "mature," or "leadership" voice.

Get rid of the artificial person you think you're supposed to be. Become the person you really are. This is about being yourself.

The real you.

When in doubt, speak even more quietly. You need only enough volume to be heard. Emphasis and energy should be added by using pitch and rate changes rather than by adding volume. Pitch and rate are the storytellers' tools.

Once up on a tiii me.

Try saying these sentences without any expression:

- She's a remarkable person.
- It was a delightful movie.
- He's a dynamite speaker.
- You believe that liar?
- It was an overwhelming experience.
- He's never done an honest day's work in his life.
- Just who does she think she is?

Open up

Get the brows up. Gesture—illustrate with a hand—on the emphasized words. Make it meaningful by making it important. The pitch and rate should follow.

Say those sentences again. It makes a huge difference, doesn't it? When you put it all together, it makes communication nothing less than a performing art. Not acting, mind you, but presenting yourself in a dynamic, interesting, attention-grabbing way.

When the mind, face, body, and voice are working together for the benefit of the audience, the end result is almost always likability, and *likability wins.*

It Works

One of my clients brought me to her staff annually. When the training was over for the department heads, she invited the receptionists, secretaries, and all the people who were early phone contacts for callers or visitors. I would work with them for half an hour on the face and voice relationship, and had them do the "good morning," exercise aloud. They were surprised to realize that the facial expression made such a dramatic difference. On one visit, a young woman named Esther sought me out and said, "Mr. Lustberg, I can't thank you enough. Since you showed me how to use my face and voice, I've been promoted three times."

Selling Your Confidence

The number-one human fear seems to be speaking before a group, so it doesn't take a rocket scientist to know that public speaking creates an enormous stress factor for a lot of people. But it's important to realize that, although stress is a communication killer, nervousness is an asset.

So the fundamental idea of this chapter is how to turn stress (bad) into nervous energy (good).

With this skill, you'll be able to develop the all-important ingredient: confidence. It really isn't a long journey from "I'm going to make an ass of myself in front of all these people," to "They came to hear what I have to say. They want me to succeed. After all, it's their time, and it's up to me to make it valuable for them. I have good information. All I need to do is make it interesting."

Care About the Audience

That frame of mind is a good introduction to converting from self-consciousness to the confidence that comes from realizing you are there for the audience, not the other way around. So, the concentration should be outward—on them—rather than inward—on you. Then, "Is my hair in place? Am I falling apart? Is my fly zipped (or is my lipstick smeared)?" becomes, "Get them with the program. Give them a dynamite opening. Relate to them. Show them you care about them." Confidence isn't cockiness.

It isn't smugness. It's the awareness that, by being audience-friendly, you're selling yourself, and you want them to be on your team.

Make Nervousness Your Ally

Nervousness is a perfectly natural and almost universal occurrence. Ask any singer, any actor, any performer. You'll hear the same thing over and over: "I'm nervous before every performance. It [nervousness] energizes my performance. It gives me the edge I need." So, don't confuse nervousness with "stage fright." Again, that's the difference between an energized presentation and a stressed-out one.

Talk to professional athletes. They'll tell you their least productive games were the ones in which they were unsure of themselves, ones in which they lacked confidence.

Think of the tension a State Department spokesperson struggles with knowing that every word might produce an international incident.

Each one of those people must deal with the same kind of pressure, tension, and stress that's placed on you as a speaker. The difference between you and those professionals is probably the confidence with which they handle their situations.

Confidence Can Be Learned

As a speaker, you're relating directly to an audience. Any group needs to believe that you seem comfortable, that you have confidence in yourself. Otherwise, they'll never be able to have confidence in your message.

Without confidence, you have:

- Fear.
- Stress.
- Tension.
- Self-consciousness.
- A rapid heartbeat that you can feel.

- Disorganized thoughts.

- Dryness (in your mouth).

- Wetness (everywhere else).

- Evident signs of discomfort.

With confidence, you have:

- Control (of self and audience).

- Comfort.

- Presence of mind to think.

- Positive nervous energy, making you dynamic.

- The ability to concentrate on your message and your audience.

Consider the following case study demonstrating the importance of confidence.

Almost immediately after attending one of my training sessions, an association executive director had to represent his industry in one of the first and most media-covered product-tampering cases.

Almost every day for several weeks he held news conferences at the Food and Drug Administration and responded to unrelenting questions from the media.

He testified before congressional committees where the TV lights blazed, cameras rolled, and questions were often hostile and intimidating. The pressure was constant.

After it was over, he told me, "Without the confidence your training gave me, I never could have handled my end of the crisis."

Of course, the product was Tylenol.

How to Gain Confidence

In anything you do, the greater your confidence in yourself and your abilities, the stronger your impact.

That's not cockiness, mind you. It's being prepared. It's knowing how to take control of your own metabolism and turn your stress into nervousness that generates enthusiasm and energy.

The Secret Key

The concept is easy to understand, but just how do you go about taking control of your metabolism? After all, your heart rate is racing. Your blood pressure is over the top.

The key is so simple, you're going to wonder if I really know what I'm talking about.

The secret to controlling stress is diaphragmatic breathing. It's the way the baby breathes when the umbilical cord is severed, meaning that it's natural breathing. If anything can be labeled "organic" or "100-percent natural," it's diaphragmatic breathing.

It's a fact. There's a way to breathe that can work against you, especially in a difficult situation, and there's a way to breathe properly that can help make that same difficult situation less stressful.

The following story is an example of how this breathing technique works. A former colleague of mine was invited to attend a luncheon at the White House. He was thrilled! Then he discovered that each guest was expected to stand and present a 60-second self-introduction in front of a roomful of high-powered guests.

His elation turned to panic. He decided not to go. I happened to hear about his decision and suggested that we work together on his breathing—only breathing—to control his panic. He decided it was worth a try. Guess what. He not only went to the luncheon, but he enjoyed it.

Another example of the effectiveness of correct breathing comes from even closer to home. One of my then-teenage children told me one evening, "I had to give an oral report in class today. I read your booklet and worked on my breathing. Everyone told me I gave the best report."

These are just two examples of how proper breathing has worked for people. There are countless others involving people in every field, from library directors testifying on behalf of their budget requests to the city council to a presidential hopeful about to make the speech to announce his candidacy.

Improper Breathing Can Be a Roadblock

Remember the speaker who kept gasping for breath and audibly sucking in air in the middle of sentences? Remember the ones who preceded every fifth word with "uh...uh...uh" until you could think of nothing but their discomfort and your own boredom? In each case you remember that you were in pain for them. But do you remember the message? Probably not.

In winter, the coughs and sneezes you suffer are usually a sign that something is wrong. You probably have a cold. You're getting sick. In much the same way, the "uh...uh...uhs" and the stammering and groping are signs that something is wrong.

That "something" is lack of control.

Lack of competence.

Lack of confidence.

They're communication killers.

Fortunately, this handicap is curable with proper breathing and silent pauses.

Assumptions to consider:

- *First:* Assume you're faced with a difficult situation, maybe even a crisis situation.

- *Second:* Of course, you want to handle it successfully.

In order to do this, you must obtain and maintain control. That means control of your stress and your thought process. You can do it with proper breathing.

Keep in mind that no good vocal coach ever let a student make the first sound until the student had mastered proper breathing techniques.

Speech 101 and Singing 101 follow this regimen if properly taught. In this case, you're your own coach, so monitor your progress carefully.

No shortcuts

There are no shortcuts, so take it slowly. You may find the progress complicated by old, improper breathing habits you've acquired over the years. You have to learn to replace them with new, correct ones you're about to develop.

Let's make sure you understand what you do when you think of taking a deep breath.

Picture this: You've gone for your annual checkup. The doctor puts a stethoscope to your chest and says, "Now take a deep breath." You suck in your gut. You swell your chest and hike up your shoulders, tightening the muscles of your head and neck as if you're a soldier at attention.

Notice the difference in the muscles of the head and neck. Chest breathing tightens and stresses.

Keep that image in mind because that's exactly what you *don't* want to do. I never saw a soldier at attention who resembled a relaxed, comfortable speaker. So, when you heave up the shoulders as you suck in the gut to take a deep breath, you're going about it the wrong way.

To learn proper breathing techniques, you first need to understand that the center of the breathing mechanism, the main muscle, is the diaphragm. It's a dome-shaped arch located just under the rib cage, right below the breastbone.

The lungs rest on the diaphragm, so when you look for your diaphragm, if you find yourself anywhere near your navel, you're too far south.

The proper breathing rhythm is for the diaphragm to flatten on inhalation.

On exhalation, the diaphragm returns to its arched position, forcing air out of the lungs by pushing them up.

Place your fingers against your diaphragm. On an inhalation, your fingers should be forced away from your body. On the exhalation, your fingers should move back toward your body.

Be very conscious of what you're doing because it's quite common to do it wrong. At first, it may seem unnatural.

Diaphragmatic breathing relaxes and normalizes.

We've been used to thinking that the "in" in "inhale" means sucking in the gut. The "in" actually means filling the lungs with air, and it can only happen when the diaphragm flattens, moving down and away from the body.

Unlearn bad breathing techniques

Incorrect breathing often comes from military training, exaggerated posture training, and an involuntary reaction to stress and fear. It goes back to the terrible notion of "take a deep breath." The command should be "take a diaphragmatic breath."

Incorrect breathing is one of the leading causes of lack of confidence.

It's a communication destroyer.

Practice correctly

Check it out. Stand in front of a mirror. Pretend you've just heard the magic words: "Take a deep breath." If you're pulling your diaphragm in, sucking in the gut, your shoulders will heave upward. The muscles of your head and neck will tighten noticeably. It's exactly the opposite of what should be happening.

Your shoulders shouldn't move on the inhalation. The lungs need room to expand. The motion of the diaphragm should be outward, not upward.

Yawning and sighing are almost perfect examples of deep diaphragmatic breathing. You're always breathing correctly lying on your back as you fall asleep.

The trouble is that you can't check on your breathing while you sleep, so in order to experience this type of breathing, try these exercises.

Exercise 1

Lie on your back. Fold your arms across your diaphragm and close your eyes. Notice that by the third or fourth breath, your breathing rhythm is normal and correct. Your diaphragm is moving away from your spine on inhalation and back toward the spine as you exhale.

It's harder to accomplish this rhythm when you're standing, so now try standing up. Place your fingers on the diaphragm. Take a gentle but forceful breath. Don't think about "deep breathing." Think about pushing out on your fingers as you inhale. Now, exhale and let your fingers return to your body. Inhale again. Push your fingers away. Return to the original inward position as you exhale. Repeat it several times.

Repetition makes perfect. Close your eyes and repeat it several more times. Notice that when you're doing it right, there's a surge of relaxed, comfortable well-being flowing through your body. Your metabolism is normalizing, moving toward peace. This is the state hypnotherapists try to induce leading up to the hypnotic state. It's the breathing method taught by yoga and meditation classes. It's taught for natural childbirth methods to help reduce the pain that's stress-related. And when in doubt, watch a sleeping baby breathe.

Exercise 2

Press the fingers of one hand into your diaphragm. Place the fingers of the other hand on the back of your neck. Take an incorrect deep, deep breath. Suck your diaphragm in hard as you inhale. Notice how tense the muscles in your head and neck have become. Your whole head is filling with tension. So is your whole body.

Now do the same thing with your hands, but correct the breathing rhythm. Push your fingers away as you inhale and let them return as you exhale. Feel the tension race out of the back of your neck. You're experiencing the first leg of your journey toward relaxation.

In maybe three or four breaths, you have your body reacting the way you want it to rather than reacting to the stress of the situation. You're controlling your body rather than letting your body control you.

Now, let your mind take over. Obviously, you can't stand up in front of your board of directors, smile, and say, "Hold it just a second, folks," then go into your breathing exercise. But you certainly can practice proper breathing techniques inconspicuously while waiting your turn to present. You can practice correct breathing anytime you're alone or anytime you're in a group when the group's focus is on someone else.

In fact, once you've mastered the technique, you can do it anywhere, anytime. If it's done right, it won't even require special finger placement. It will feel right and be inconspicuous. Now your mind can take over.

I also recommend practicing your breathing on the telephone. Most of us spend a tremendous amount of time on the phone. It's a great time to put the free hand on the diaphragm and "make it happen." It won't be long before you're breathing correctly all the time.

Don't Let Stress Destroy Your Control

All bets are off when stress strikes. When the guillotine is about to fall, just about everyone tends to breathe improperly and tighten everything.

Think about scenarios such as these:

- You're furious because a colleague just single-handedly lost your biggest client with a stupid, thoughtless, avoidable act.

- One of your children just totaled your car in a careless accident. He's okay—no injury, but now all you can think of is the stupidity of the act.

- Your mayor just announced that the city is doubling your real-estate tax.

- You're in a true state of road rage.

In situations such as these, *stop*. Take several diaphragmatic breaths. Let your breathing help you get hold of yourself. Let your breathing force the tension out of your body and soothe you back into comfort and control.

Recognize Stress for What It Is

The problem, of course, is realizing you're in a stressful state when you're in it. Usually, extreme stress is so extreme it takes over and we're unaware of anything else. It's vitally important that you learn how to recognize when you're in deep stress. Otherwise, you won't be able to control it because you won't have the presence of mind to concentrate on letting your breathing help release you from the prison of stress.

I know it's hard to concentrate on a physical act such as breathing when your body wants to perform a physical act more along the lines of murder, but the more you let panic reign, the harder it is to throw it off.

So, once again, proper breathing is basic to good communication. It's fundamental.

Good spoken communication begins with good breathing. Self-control is the name of the game.

It Works!

If you suffer the pangs of fear and stress when you know you're going to speak, read what two of the people I've trained who felt the same way you do have said:

"When I feel a panic attack coming on, I stop, take two or three dia-phragmatic breaths, and I'm back in command of myself and my situation."

"I'm convinced that breathing is the most important lesson I got. I'm much more in control of myself. It really amazes me to be able to be confi-dent in what used to be a bad situation."

Even the most experienced speakers have told me that proper breath-ing before—and during—their presentation is the vital ingredient in deliv-ering their message with confidence.

Michael D. Bradbury, district attorney of Ventura County, California, wrote me:

> As I remember my interview on ABC's *20/20,* when hit with some tough questions, I recalled your sage advice. I took my time, along with a couple of deep diaphragmatic breaths, and came up with some memorable remarks.

When you have self-confidence, your audience will have confidence in you. They'll like you better, and likability wins.

elling With the Right Signals

Everything you do sends signals to the people you're talking to. You've watched presenters who tug at an ear every five seconds. You've seen people presenting who have a dry mouth and are constantly moistening their lips. You've watched people who look as though they wish they were anywhere else—so does the audience.

Send the Right Signals

The important message here is that you can learn how to send the proper signals that help the audience find you competent, confident, and likable.

Some people call it "body language."

Some call it "non-verbal communication."

I call it "sending signals."

I've already talked about how breathing can send signals.

If your audience watches your shoulders heave upward as you inhale, you look tight, tense, stiff, and intimidated. You may not be aware that you're doing it, but your audience will be, and they will read those signals as "uncomfortable," and soon they, too, will be uncomfortable.

Everything About You Sends a Signal

The way you use your face, your hands, and your voice sends signals. What you wear sends signals. So does your general appearance, your grooming. In short, as long as your audience can see you, what they see is as important as what you say.

The combination of the neutral face and a position such as the fig leaf has the audience thinking, "This poor person!" They realize you're not pleased to be there and that you've got problems, and they'll wish they were somewhere else.

Sending Good Signals

In any speaking situation, your job is to help the audience receive the message you want them to get, but it's not as simple as it sounds. It means that they have to perceive you to be comfortable, confident, and in control, whether you're standing behind a lectern, sitting at a conference table, or simply in conversation.

Standing Isn't as Easy as It Sounds

The position a lot of people find least comfortable is standing with their hands at their sides. Interestingly and unfortunately, this is the most comfortable position for the audience to see. It looks natural. It sends the most friendly, open, personable signals, but most of us find the hands naked. We don't like to be naked, so we hide the hands. By giving in to this impulse, we wind up in an awkward-looking position. Most men go right for the fig leaf. Most women fold their arms in front of them. Of course, some thrust their hands in their pockets and others hide their hands behind their backs.

None of these stances look comfortable or inviting to an audience. Worse still, these positions are gesture inhibitors, meaning we're unable to "hug" an audience or "shake hands" via the gesture. Each of the "no-no" positions sends signals that usually will be interpreted by an audience as signs of stiffness or insecurity. Yet, time after time, people automatically assume one of these hand-hiding positions.

There are many examples of this. Look at photographs of award ceremonies, company meetings, and social functions. Nearly everyone will be in the fig-leaf or arms-folded position. Look at a newspaper picture of the president, governor, or mayor signing a bill or holding a press conference. All the aides and participants will be in an uncomfortable-looking position in the background. It almost looks posed. It's almost comical.

What you can learn is how to send the signals that show your audience you're comfortable, in control, and self-confident.

How to stand

When standing, I recommend this position:

- Erect posture.

- Feet about shoulder-width apart.

- One foot slightly in front of the other.

- Hands comfortably at your sides; fingers quiet and relaxed.

- Head erect.

- Chin up but not exaggerated.

Here are the messages you'll send in this position:

- An erect posture suggests authority.

- Feet spread suggest solidity.

- One foot slightly forward lets you move toward the audience as you gesture. It suggests the embrace and the hug I spoke of earlier.

- With your hands at your sides you look natural and comfortable.

- Keeping your head erect with your chin up prevents you from looking as if you're talking down to your audience—or worse, from looking down your nose at your audience—or from tilting your head to one side.

I've noticed that many people tilt their heads to one side. I think it weakens the communication. I realize there are coaches who think the tilted head looks good. I don't agree. Your head should be erect and still.

I stress "still" because many people react with head nods instead of using the open face. Often, we nod as we're listening intently. It says, "I agree." But in many cases, the nod is habit and even though we mean it to say, "I understand where you're coming from," what we're reacting to is an accusation of wrongdoing or bad thinking and the audience sees, "You're absolutely right." It looks bad.

What to do with your hands. Once you're comfortable with the right way to stand, take a couple of diaphragmatic breaths. Shake out your shoulders. See where your hands fall naturally. They should be at your sides.

Fingers that fidget, clutch at things, or are fully extended won't look comfortable to an audience. So avoid the temptation to wiggle the fingers or tug at the bottom of your jacket. Your fingers should be slightly curled, with the thumb angled slightly toward the audience.

Don't let either your palm or the back of your hand face the audience.

Stay loose and gesture. What has been illustrated so far is only your starting position. I don't recommend that you stand as still as a statue. Use gestures to punctuate what you're saying and to help the audience visualize what you're saying. After the first few gestures, you'll find that your hands can come to lots of other positions and look good.

- Your fingers can be folded gently in front of you.
- One hand can move to a pocket after a gesture.
- Your arms can be folded in front if you'll come out of it to gesture and then return to another position.

It's important to vary the gestures so that they're genuine and appropriate. It's also important to vary the hand positions.

Whatever subsequent positions you choose, keep in mind that the gesture is one of the strong signals you send.

The open face says, "I care." The gesture says, "I share," "This communication is important to me," and "I hug you with this idea."

Keep up the good work. Keep using your hands and your arms to make appropriate and genuine gestures. Don't succumb to the temptation to hide them. You'll also discover that by varying the hand you use to gesture, you'll help yourself vary the gestures.

For some reason I don't understand, television personalities are discouraged from using their hands. It's created some really weird communication styles. The reporters, anchors, and talking heads speak with heads bobbing, shoulder-jerking, and odd movements for emphasis. We all talk with our hands, so all those other awkward wriggles are gesture-substitutes that look weird.

The lectern

The same principles apply to the lectern. You can hold it with both hands, but don't clutch it. Clutching the lectern tightly is the podium equivalent of the fig leaf. Use the lectern, but not as a crutch. Don't become dependent on it to hold you up.

When you are standing behind a lectern, use natural and appropriate gestures. They don't have to be big. The audience doesn't even have to see them, but using them gives you energy. It pumps you up. It helps you embrace your audience. I like to recommend offering the audience a hand movement on the initial greeting, such as, "Good morning." It brings presenter and audience together.

Sitting

Sitting is usually an easier communication position than standing, but it can be more tricky and deceptive. This is because we're likely to feel more comfortable sitting, even though we often look less comfortable.

We like to sit back when we're relaxed.

We often let ourselves "sink in."

Sofas and easy chairs that swivel and lean back especially tend to trap us. When we lean back, sink in, or swivel, we appear to lose interest in the person with whom we're talking or the person to whom we should be listening. When someone is leaning, sinking, or swiveling, you're getting a signal that he or she is uninterested in the communication.

There are many ways to appear disinterested when sitting, such as looking stiff and uncomfortable.

...or leaning back with legs spread apart. (TV calls this the "crotch shot.")

I remember William F. Buckley when he had a regularly scheduled television show. He leaned so far back in his chair that he seemed completely uninterested in his guest. Worse, the audience got the impression of a supremely inflated ego and that he was looking down his nose at an inferior.

How to sit

If you lean back, you're likely to send the signal that you just don't care about what you're saying or with whom you're talking.

When you're alone or surrounded by people who know you well, any position is fine; but when you're trying to make a favorable impression, or when an audience, a colleague, or a client is looking at you, I recommend these techniques:

...or checking your watch.   *...or looking away.*

- Sit with your spine erect but not exaggerated.

- Lean slightly forward.

- Keep your knees together.

- If you cross your legs, cross the top at a downward angle. The least attractive part of your wardrobe is the sole of your shoe, so why put it on display?

- Have your hands in a comfortable position and free to gesture.

- Keep your spine away from the back of the chair. Resist the temptation to slump.

- If the chair has arms, your arms can rest on them, but don't let your hands dangle. Your hands may touch the chair's arms, but don't clutch them. You can rest your hands on your thighs if you prefer. If you fold your hands on your lap, leave them loose and free to gesture.

The only way to sit is to look interested with good posture and an open face.

Sitting erect and leaning slightly forward with an open face as you speak will always send the right signals.

How to React

I realize that this isn't about acting, but I think you should know that any trained actor would tell you that a considerable percentage of acting is reacting. The same is true of communication. Much of being a good communicator is being a good listener. You're sending signals even when you're not speaking.

Think about the many head-table people you've watched in your lifetime who seem to ignore the keynote speaker.

Think about all the panel members you've seen who haven't bothered to look at the panelist who's speaking and give the appearance they're just bored with the whole thing.

We've all watched the vice president and Speaker of the House seemingly wishing they were somewhere else during the State of the Union address.

When you're not speaking, you're still "on"

My point is that when you're not speaking, you have to stay alert and look interested because the audience may be looking at you. In fact, if you aren't responding, you'll probably be distracting the audience. Your reactions must be as genuine and appropriate as your smile and the gesture.

Sitting in the audience at dinner meetings, I'm amazed at how many head-table people, often celebrities or business or political leaders, will look at their watches, sip coffee, stare straight ahead, or even talk to each other while someone else is presenting.

The audience is being distracted, and attention is literally being stolen from the person they should be listening to.

Be a good listener

Listening is as important to a career as learning to speak well. Communication isn't complete without both. And here, too, a sure sign of interest, caring, and attentive listening is the open face.

Some of the most universally seen listeners and reactors are the first ladies. Almost any picture we've ever seen of any first family shows the first lady listening and reacting to the president. First ladies are almost never seen looking anywhere else when their husbands are speaking. Sometimes we're troubled that they seem to look too adoringly at their husbands, but even if it looks staged, it helps keep the audience's focus.

Sending signals in conversation

I'll never forget a moment when a friend met me on the street. He was totally surprised and seemed really pleased to see me. His face lit up. His voice sang out, "Hi, Arch. It's great to see you again." It was a wonderful greeting, but in the next instant, he remembered that he hadn't been feeling well that morning. His eyes narrowed, his jaw dropped, and his shoulders drooped. In a mournful voice, he asked me, "Do I look tired to you?" He certainly did. He sent the exact signals he meant to send, but they didn't seem appropriate.

This is an example of how signals are just as important in one-on-one communication as in groups.

After all, we're usually talking to one other person, not a group. The public or group speaking situation is quite infrequent.

Yet, much too often in one-on-one communication, one person tells another, "That's not what you said" or "I don't remember you saying that."

In all probability, some of the signals were wrong and it caused misunderstanding, which then caused miscommunication.

We're Sending Signals All the Time

Signal-sending and receiving touches every facet of our lives. Consider the doctor-patient relationship. It's called "bedside manner." Have you heard people say, "He's too busy. He doesn't really care. I'm just another patient to him"? He probably does care. After all, the doctor's job is to "care" for people. Many are simply unaware of how to send the signals that say, "I care," other than to simply treat the illness.

Think about the signals in the office environment: the boss-employee relationship and those between colleagues. Think about the signals in the parent-child and teacher-student relationships. More often than not, interpersonal problems are caused by misunderstood signals rather than by misunderstood words.

The words we choose, the way we say them, and the way we look all have an important bearing on the signals we send. It doesn't really matter what we say if it doesn't reach the person who hears it the way we intended.

Clothing

In addition to your face and your posture, your clothes send signals even before you've said a word.

The 1990s brought dramatic changes. The dotcom surge, the Silicon Valley explosion, changed everything in a big way. But, even though the uniform-of-the-day—blue suit, white shirt, subdued tie—is over for a while, certain rules still apply.

The local bank manager is still out of place in cutoff jeans.

An employee of the Department of Agriculture who works in farm country can't make it in a three-piece suit carrying a leather attaché case.

Shirts open to the navel with gold chains hanging down over the bare chest won't make it at the brokerage house or IBM.

Let common sense rule

Today there are very few rules. Casual Friday has cloned itself to include six other days in most places. The guiding principle is compatibility. Clothing has to blend with the situation and the audience's expectations.

My rule is that nothing you do and nothing you wear should attract unnecessary attention.

Anything that's noticed about you can destroy your message.

Anything that's conspicuous will interrupt, interfere with, or cancel out your communication.

You want the audience to leave with your message, not the memory of a mustard stain on your shirt.

Mark Twain said, "Clothes make the man. Naked people have little or no influence on society." Well, neither do inappropriately dressed people. Clothes should fit well, look comfortable, and be appropriate for the occasion.

I also think you're at your best when you feel comfortable in what you're wearing. I don't function as well in a heavily starched shirt collar, so I don't wear starched shirts. Do what works for you.

I remember the book *Dress for Success* had a warning to businesspeople that brown was out—until Ronald Reagan appeared regularly in brown suits. He looked terrific, and brown made a triumphant return. The colors you choose should look good and help you feel good about yourself.

I like leaving the question of the buttoning of the jacket to you and your comfort factor. I hate watching the politician get up, start to walk to the microphone, and automatically button the jacket. It looks robotic. Here again, whatever works best for you is usually easiest on the eye.

Looking good while seated

When you're sitting, it's usually best to leave the jacket unbuttoned. Television anchors are about the only ones who look as though their clothes were tailored for the sitting position. Most of us wind up looking as if we left the hanger in the jacket when we put it on that morning. Seated, the jacket tends to crawl up in back, and the top of the jacket winds up a couple of inches above the shirt collar. It looks sloppy.

The film *Broadcast News* had a wonderful scene showing how the tail of the jacket is pulled down and sat on to keep the collar from traveling up.

Bare Skin Will Get All the Attention

Bare skin that isn't supposed to be bare is distracting. Bare skin is for the beach. We should never see more than we ought to see from the speaker in any professional situation.

Bare skin is a no-no. It stops the message cold.

For men, I advise long-sleeved shirts and over-the-calf socks.

When short-sleeved shirts are appropriate, it's probably also appropriate to shed the jacket, but a lot of bare arm under the jacket sleeve looks underdressed, if not undressed. The same goes for socks. We don't want to see the skin under the trouser leg.

Women should wear blouses buttoned high; at least above the line where the cleavage begins, and, in public appearances, no slit skirts or mini-skirts, please. The people in your audience shouldn't be encouraged to take physical inventory when they should be concentrating on your message. It will be a long time before people forget the fuss that Hillary Clinton caused during the '08 campaign when she appeared on the Senate floor in a blouse that revealed a bit of cleavage.

If the room is likely to be overheated, take off your jacket or sweater before you enter the room. There's something suggestive of a stripper when you take off clothes in public. The act of removing clothes also tends to highlight the curves of the form, and that always calls attention.

Dress up, not down.

Jewelry

The same rules apply to jewelry. In social situations, almost anything goes, but when you're in the spotlight, your audience shouldn't be aware of your jewelry. Anything that catches the eye (or the ear, for that matter) tends to distract and make it harder for the audience to stay with the message. Your jewelry should be subdued for professional or presentation situations.

Some women don't realize that dangling earrings move with even the slightest head movement. The object in motion captures the eyes and, fascinated by the side-to-side, hypnotic movement of earrings, the audience loses sight of what the speaker is saying.

Because we watch the object in motion, the only really appropriate moves are speaker moves—gestures and steps taken to vary the physical position. These should be natural, appropriate, and genuine so the audience isn't aware of them.

Also, keep in mind that heavy, expensive-looking, glittery, or ostentatious jewelry that may be appropriate in the social setting won't work on the platform.

As a general rule, no audience wants to be aware of how expensively or ornately you're dressed or bejeweled. It can be a huge turnoff. Take the following story, for example.

A group of people were attending a training session to prepare them to present an appeal to a foundation for funding. They were looking for a grant of several million dollars to help people restore homes in run-down neighborhoods. It would be a model program and was a truly worthwhile request.

The sponsoring organization felt that it would be most effective to have the appeal made by "real people"—neighborhood residents and business owners—rather than by bureaucrats. It was a brilliant concept. Who better to plead the case than the people whose lives would be improved by the grant? These were the people who were involved, interested, and filled with passion for the project.

As the training progressed, I noticed that one of the women was wearing a set of gold bracelets that went from her wrist to her elbow. I suggested that she remove them for the presentation. She shot me a withering look and said, "These bracelets never leave my arm."

I'm not sure that was one of the contributing reasons why the grant was denied, but the moral of the story is this: Blatant jewelry displays should be reserved for the people who make it part of their mystique, such as movie celebrities parading for the cameras on Oscar night.

Don't Make It Hard for Yourself

Again, communication means moving what's in your mind easily and directly into the mind of the recipient. Anything that gets in the way of that movement, the intellectual and emotional movement, tends to destroy the communication. The person in the audience who isn't aware of what you're wearing, how you're standing or sitting, or what you're doing, is free to concentrate on what you're saying.

All the signals you send should be communication signals, not personal ones. Allow your audience to get what you intend it to get: what's on your mind.

Selling Yourself as a Speaker

There are three factors to consider in any speaking situation:

- The logistics.
- What to do.
- How to do it.

Many people waste an enormous amount of time and energy on negative thoughts, such as:

- I never should have agreed to do it.
- I'm going to bomb.
- I'll never have enough time to prepare.
- I won't be able to come up with a decent idea.
- If I keep doing this, I'll shorten my life by 20 years.
- I wonder if I can cancel.
- I'm not going to be able to sleep.

Stop it!

All you are doing is building a wall between you and a really good presentation.

The Logistics

Here are some of the questions you need to ask your host and yourself:

- Why me?

- What do you want me to talk about? (But be prepared for a response of "anything you want.")

- Who's my audience?

- How do I fit in into the rest of the program? Is there an overall theme to the meeting?

- Where and when will I speak?

- Who is my contact when I have questions about time, room set-up, arrival, transportation, and ground rules?

- How much time have you set aside for me? Will you consider less time?

Finalize these arrangements before accepting the assignment and before sitting down to write word one.

Why Me?

What do I know—or what do they think I know—that will enlighten the audience? You may not have an international reputation, but you were invited to speak. Find out why they invited you. It may suggest an innovative introduction or even suggest a topic if they don't care about your topic.

What Do They Want Me to Talk About?

The importance of the topic should be obvious from the start. If they want you to talk about international terrorism and you know nothing about it, obviously you're not the right speaker for them. Don't agree to speak. That should be a no-brainer, but some very bright people have made the mistake of agreeing to speak before finding out if there was a specific assignment in mind.

A friend of mine (one of the best speakers I've ever worked with) was asked by her local chamber of commerce to appear on a program. She's a successful entrepreneur and was prepared to speak on many subjects involved in starting and building a business.

It was too late when she found out that they were doing a series on employee benefits. That wasn't her area of expertise. In fact, it wasn't a subject that even interested her. Someone else, an extremely capable person, handled that area for her company.

She should have sent that other person, but she went and admitted later that it was a mistake.

Who's the Audience?

No matter what the subject is, you have to know who the audience is. If there's no specified topic, the audience is even more important. The makeup of the audience may inspire a subject.

Do they have a common interest?

Do they represent a single profession?

I often sit through a presentation that precedes one of mine.

One time the presenter was a "motivational" speaker and was firing up the audience with a "gung-ho—go get 'em" message. Then he told them their job was to get out there and destroy the competition. The problem was that his audience was all staff of a public utility. They had no competition. Once the audience realized they were listening to a "canned" speech being delivered for the 500th time and that the speaker didn't take the trouble to tailor the message to them, they turned him off.

Make sure your message has something special for this audience: a new perspective, an innovation—something that adds to their body of knowledge or understanding—something that gives them an incentive to listen to you.

How and Where Do I Fit?

Are you the only speaker?

Is there a marching band playing walk-in music and then the national anthem before you come on?

Are you the third of four speakers?

Will the program chair keep all the speakers on schedule?

Who are the other speakers, and what are their topics?

What's on the agenda before your talk (a luncheon), during your talk (waiters clearing tables), after your talk (questions)?

Who's introducing you?

What kind of introduction will it be?

You may not be able to get all the answers on the first call, but keep asking. The better your information, the better your chances of making a strong, relevant, effective presentation.

Is There a Theme?

A lot of meetings and conventions are given "grabber" titles. Make a special effort to include that title and relevant information inside your message.

Where and When Will I Speak?

The site is very important. If you've spoken in this room or auditorium a lot, you'll feel almost as comfortable as you are in your living room. If it's on the 50-yard line at the Super Bowl game, you're on foreign soil. You always should consider an on-site rehearsal and always, always check your equipment beforehand.

Who's My Contact?

This can often be the most important question you ask. No one can make you look better or worse than the meeting planner, and nothing is more frustrating than having a problem and not knowing who can help. Things are bound to come up that weren't anticipated. Find out right away who's assigned to "hold your hand."

My rule is simple:

> If the audience doesn't know you have a problem,
> you don't have a problem.

How Much Time Do I Have?

People who book speakers often want the most time they can get. For them, it becomes a matter of quantity instead of quality. Above all, you must never lose sight of the audience and remember the old vaudeville adage: Always leave them wanting more.

They should feel sorry, not relieved, that it's over.

Other Points to Consider

The physical set-up

- The size and shape of the room.

- The location of the audience in relation to you, the speaker.

- Will the room be set theater-style, classroom-style, or at round tables?

- The location and quality of the microphones.

- The height of the lectern. (Short people shouldn't hesitate to ask for a solid box to stand on.)

- The setting of the stage: head table, lots of gadgetry and equipment for other speakers' visuals.

- The lighting in relation to your ability to see your text, outline, or notes.

- Don't leave any room for surprises.

The occasion

If you're expected to be hilarious (a roast) or touching (a memorial service), you'd better know about it in advance. This may seem ridiculous and far-fetched, but I know people who were shocked to realize at the last minute that the remarks they had prepared were totally inappropriate for the situation.

The format

You can choose to speak from a prepared text, an outline, notes, or nothing. I urge you to pick what works best for you. But whatever format you choose, start by preparing a text. It will help a lot. It gives you the chance to look at it, change it, shape it, give it form, and practice it. And remember: It isn't beyond belief that someone will ask you for a copy of your speech.

The length

When you like your text a lot, cut it by a third. Keep it short and simple. Today's attention span is limited.

The style

Write conversational sentences. Great literature rarely makes great speeches. And keep in mind that speeches are meant to be spoken, not read. That may sound foolish, but I assure you it isn't. Take a look at a book of great speeches and see how false many of the words sound when you say them out loud.

Preparing and Delivering Your Words
Write for the Ear!

Make sure the words sound the way they sound in animated conversation. Get rid of jargon, "governmentese," legalese, insider language, and acronyms. Look at a section of the *Federal Register* (the publication that transcribes the speeches delivered on the floor of Congress) and you'll get a lesson in how not to write a speech.

"It is incumbent upon us to ensure that the obfuscatory nature of formal discourse be dispensed with in the most propitious manner." This quote really says, "Simplify your language." It's amazing how many of us make the mistake of trying to impress an audience with our brilliance while forgetting to express ourselves clearly, simply, briefly, and unforgettably.

How about this one:

> *Serving as a panelist with the other past presidents of the [association name] is indeed a pleasure and a rare opportunity. It is hard to believe that a 10-year span of time has passed since our first session. What perspectives the*

*various past presidents have brought to the hundreds of
people who have attended our sessions through the years!"*

I'm sure that those words felt perfectly natural to the person writing
them as he was putting them on paper, but they certainly don't "talk like
conversation." If you don't edit the garbage of "a 10-year span of time" to
"10 years," you'll trip over your words at the lectern and, worse, you'll run
the risk of being perceived as a windbag. And remember: Nobody loves a
windbag—not even another windbag.

Do yourself and your audience a favor. Convert flowery language into
simple, everyday conversation:

> *"I can't believe it's been 10 years since our first session!
> It's great to serve here with the other past presidents. Each
> has brought a unique perspective."*

Short Sentences Are Winners

On the podium, long sentences will get you in trouble. They'll force
you to look at your text and read when you should be looking at your audience and talking.

I've seen speech texts with sentences of 60 words and up.

Let's look at one with a mere 28:

> *"Those costs and the inconvenience to airline passengers
> can be reduced substantially, but fundamental changes in
> the funding and management of our air traffic control
> system are required."*

Sentences such as that can be edited and reconstructed into shorter,
more dynamic, easier-to-deliver sentences. The audience might even go
away remembering the message if it were presented this way:

> *"We could cut those costs. We could reduce the
> inconvenience to the passengers. But we'd have to make
> some changes, basic changes, in the way we fund and
> manage air traffic control."*

Simple Language Is a Winner

A talk that uses simple language is easy to give, it's easy to follow, and it's easy to understand. An audience that stops to think about definitions, grammar, syntax, and vague imagery invariably falls behind the speaker and loses the next thought.

Forget statistics. Lists of numbers belong in telephone directories. Your job is to talk in unforgettable terms: stories, anecdotes, examples, and figures of speech that will paint word pictures for them and help them understand instantly. I call it "becoming your own best visual aid." People relate to you when you're using these "unforgettables."

In one of my workshops, a participant delivered this humdinger as the training began:

> *"Proposals submitted by offerors in response to the agency's RFP HSCS-6 for an information management system were examined by the agency evaluation team in order to determine that 100 percent of the mandatory requirements, considered paramount to the adequate function of the system to fulfill basic agency needs, had been met; and secondly to estimate the offerors' ability to meet the evaluated optional features, as were set forth in the above mentioned RFP. It was determined by the evaluation team, using the stated evaluation guidelines, that XYZ Corporation (he named the company) was not in a position to provide the important, if not mandatory, evaluated optional features."*

After training, he changed it to:

> *"Buying a computer system isn't that different from buying a car. First, you go to a few dealers and look at their cars. Then, you check the options you want.*
>
> *Yes, XYZ Corporation did meet the mandatory requirements. Yes, their car had four wheels, an engine, and a steering wheel, but it didn't have windshield wipers and the doors didn't lock!"*

You have more stories to share than you realize. Sharing them is the surest way to deliver a memorable speech.

An audience usually remembers well-told, relevant stories about people similar to themselves, as long as the stories amplify the point. Politicians are in love with stories about Lincoln, Jefferson, and Kennedy. If they're appropriate and told well, they work. If they aren't, they're corny and they backfire.

Never Make a Speech Again

Talk, converse, chat with a group of people. All spoken communication should be rooted in conversation.

If you need a role model, try Winston Churchill. He can teach you a lot about true eloquence.

> *We shall not flag or fail.*
>
> *We shall go on to the end.*
>
> *We shall fight in France.*
>
> *We shall fight on the seas and oceans.*
>
> *We shall fight with growing confidence and growing strength in the air.*
>
> *We shall defend our island whatever the cost may be.*
>
> *We shall fight on the beaches.*
>
> *We shall fight in the fields, and on the streets.*
>
> *We shall fight in the hills.*
>
> *We shall never surrender.*

That's the way to write a speech.

Clear.

Concise.

Conversational.

And remember: If you don't have the time or knowledge to do a decent job, don't accept the speaking assignment.

If you agree to speak, *prepare.*

Your audience deserves your best shot.

Adapt Your Speech to the Time of Day

You already know you should keep your speech short and simple because an audience's attention span is limited. You should also determine the length based on the time of day you'll deliver your talk.

A very good rule of thumb is this: The later the hour, the shorter the material.

Most people in the real world are up at 6 or 7 a.m. They work all day. They attend meetings. They work on numerous projects. Their energy and concentration levels are running low as evening approaches. If you're speaking in the early evening or after dinner, limit your speech to 10 or 15 minutes, and try to give it plenty of energy.

What about making a speech in the morning? You'll have an audience that's fresh and energetic, so you can probably hold their attention for 30 minutes if you're dynamic.

Luncheon programs are still another thing. People are usually satiated and relaxed after a luncheon, and are not as willing to listen to a speaker as at other times. It's usually best to keep your speech to a maximum of 20 minutes. They'll thank you for being considerate. You can't lose if you strictly limit yourself.

If possible, consider adding a question-and-answer period to luncheon or dinner speeches. This pumps some energy into your talk and gives the audience an opportunity to interact. Of course, some subjects and some rooms are not appropriate for question-and-answer sessions. You must judge that in advance.

Be Prompt

Always start on time. Why punish those people who made it a point to be punctual? If a break is scheduled, do your best to break promptly and resume on time. Breaks are dangerous because the refreshments and social atmosphere are terribly tempting. Ask your host or your staff to start rounding up your audience a couple of minutes before you're scheduled to continue.

The Rhythm of Eye Contact

In Chapter 2 I spoke about eye contact involving situations that were predominantly one on one. For platform presentation I've developed a technique I call "the rhythm of eye contact." It's a surefire way to connect with the audience.

Your mouth should never be moving when your eyes are down.

Your mouth should never be moving while your eyes are looking down at your text or notes, when your eyes are focused on a projected visual aid, or when you're looking at any inanimate object.

It's remarkable how effective you'll become when you look at your audience as you dramatically deliver your

...or up...

idea. In fact, it's the reason technology has developed the TelePrompTer. It's a device to help a presenter deliver every word directly to the camera.

...or on any inanimate object.

"How long do I have to continue to talk to these people?"

This is accomplished because the text of the speech rolls by on a screen between the speaker and the camera lens.

The more eye contact, the less aware the audience is of the text and the more likely it is to get the message.

Remember the four possible ways to prepare:

- Manuscript.
- Outline.
- Notes.
- Nothing.

The manuscript is the most difficult to deliver well. If you can learn the rhythm of eye contact for a manuscript speech, you'll improve the delivery of speeches prepared with any other method. So we'll concentrate on learning how to maintain eye contact while delivering the toughest speech of all.

The first rule is: Your mouth shouldn't be moving while your eyes are looking at anything but your audience.

Talking to slides or a PowerPoint presentation should be a felony.

The second rule follows logically: Write short sentences. The longest sentence should cover no more than two lines of type.

Use a large font. The type should be big. Use periods. Substitute periods for other punctuation.

I'm not saying you must write only simple sentences. I'm saying you should simplify your sentences.

Here are some other useful tips for preparing your text:

- Leave an extra-wide left-hand margin.
- Double-space your lines and triple- or quadruple-space your paragraphs. In fact, make every sentence a new paragraph and *indent.*
- Don't carry a sentence over to the next page. In other words, every page should end with a period.
- Leave a high bottom margin.
- Cut off the text about two-thirds of the way down the page.

Using the preceding two paragraphs as an example, here's how I recommend putting your text on paper. If it looks this way, you'll be making your job a lot easier.

- Write short sentences.
- The longest sentence should cover no more than two lines of type.
- Use large type.
- Use periods.
- Substitute periods for other punctuation.

Again, I'm not saying you must write simple sentences.

I'm saying *simplify* your sentences.

What on earth am I doing here?

Now let's try that text using the rhythm of eye contact. Look at the audience as you deliver each sentence from the text. Pause and look down when you come to each period. See what the next idea is. Then look up and deliver that thought. When you've completely finished the thought to the audience, pause again. Look down in silence. When the next thought is firmly in your mind, look up. Don't start until you're looking at someone, and then deliver the whole idea to the audience.

Here goes: Say the emphasized sentences to the audience. Use the italicized text to look down and get the next thought.

- **Write short sentences.**

   Pause. Look down. See the next thought. Now look up and say:

- **No sentence should cover more than two lines of type.**

   Pause. Look down. Pick up the next sentence. Look up and say:

- **Use periods.**

   Pause. Don't say anything until you're ready to look up and say:

- **Substitute periods for other punctuation.**

   Pause. Look down. See what you're going to say next. Then look up and say:

- **I'm not saying you must write simple sentences.**

   Pause. Look down. Look up and say:

- **I'm saying simplify your sentences.**

I'm sure it doesn't seem natural to you yet. It feels forced.

Practice, practice, practice!

Go back and try it again a couple of times. See if it doesn't start to feel better.

Keep trying it. In fact, try it out on a friend. Notice that each time you do it, it gets a bit smoother. It flows a little easier. Each time is a rehearsal. It will flow even better and faster when the thoughts are your thoughts instead of mine. Whatever you do, don't get discouraged. It's taken the best speakers I've trained time to get used to this technique. It's new. It's strange. But it works.

Here's another series of sentences I'd like you to try in order to get the hang of it.

- **Your mouth should never move when your eyes are down.**
  Pause. Look down. Look up and say:

- **That's a 10-word sentence.**
  Pause. Look down. Look up and say:

- **It's not necessary to look at the page.**
  Pause. Look down. Look up and say:

- **You can pause.**
  Pause. Look down. Look up and say:

- **Then you look down.**
  Pause. Look down. Look up and say:

- **The next sentence is short.**
  Pause. Look down. Look up and say:

- **So you can speak the thoughts to the audience.**
  Pause. Look down. Look up and say:

- **Instead of reading to the page.**

Speaking Situations Encountered Throughout Your Career

Introducing a Speaker

Most executives will eventually have to introduce a speaker. Although not the most difficult of speaking tasks, it still requires a certain amount of skill.

Most people make the classic mistake of reading the speaker's biography verbatim, just the way they received it in the mail. You already know that you shouldn't read anything. Now I'm here to tell you that in this situation, you shouldn't recite statistics—educational, professional, or personal—from a resume.

It's boring and ineffective.

The savvy person will request a biography well in advance. If the speaker is well known, go on the Web or to a library and do a little research. Look for interesting tidbits the audience would like to know about the speaker.

If the speaker is not well known, call or write him and conduct an informal interview to gather the same information. A person who introduces a speaker with bits of information relevant to the topic of the speech will start the session off on the right foot.

As for the resume itself, select the highlights of the speaker's career, particularly those highlights that relate specifically to the interests of the audience.

- Be selective. The audience doesn't need to know every detail of the speaker's educational and professional background.
- Be brief.
- Give highlights.
- Make the audience want to hear the speaker you're introducing.

Keep in mind that personalized stories make the best introduction—especially personalized stories that relate in some way to the talk the audience is waiting to hear. They'll mean a lot more than a list of degrees, professional credits, and other accomplishments.

It's easier to tell an audience a story than it is to read from a list.

If you don't have a personal story to tell, why not tell the audience why you selected the speaker or why you're proud to have him at your meeting?

Again, keep it brief.

A 10-minute introduction of any kind will turn virtues into vices. You'll turn the audience off before the speaker has a chance to utter a word.

Knowing what you now know about the deadly "resume introduction," and knowing that most people don't know how to make an effective introduction, why not write one for yourself? When you're asked to send a biography for introduction purposes, send your most interesting version. I know your audience will appreciate it. Maybe, together, we can start an introduction revolution.

Finally, end every introduction with the speaker's name. Make certain you articulate clearly and, please, *pronounce the name correctly*.

Serving on a Panel

You're serving on a panel. Or—even better—you're going to moderate a panel. Again, there are specifics that you must remember to effectively communicate with your audience.

First, never forget, even for a minute, that you're part of a group. Don't cut yourself short, but don't hog the spotlight either.

Second, keep your remarks noteworthy but concise. You don't have the flexibility you have when you're alone at the podium. You have to edit yourself.

You can't tell an audience everything in a few minutes. Just give the most basic, fundamental information. Skilled speakers can improvise on-site. You shouldn't take the chance. Edit in advance. Then, rehearse in front of a mirror. If you have time, practice with a colleague or a friend.

There are a number of other pointers that you'll want to remember:

▣ ***Make eye contact.*** Always look at the person to whom you're speaking.

- If you're moderating, making introductions, or talking to the audience, look at the audience.

- If you're talking to or about the panelist, look at that person and gesture in his direction.

- If someone else is talking, look at him. Don't project the feeling of boredom or frustration when someone else is talking.

- Don't let your eyes wander.

◘ *Listen intently.* You may want to react to comments and statements made by other speakers.

- Keep a pencil and paper handy so you can jot down ideas or thoughts you want to bring up later in the discussion.

- A problem can arise when another panelist continually interrupts you just as you're about to make your point. Try to avoid that situation altogether by making your point quickly and concisely. But if that doesn't work, try saying something such as, "I know they want to hear this or they wouldn't have invited me here," and then finish up as quickly as possible.

- Don't hog the program, but don't be a patsy either.

Some Final Reminders

Be yourself

You have nothing to prove. The fact that *you're* the speaker says all that needs to be said about your competence. The first major mistake most people make is trying to *look* competent, in charge, leader-like. A look back at any presidential debate leading up to the nominations shows a group of people trying to act as if they're the new commander-in-chief. They played a part and played it badly. The great irony is that Ronald Reagan, an actor, was able to be comfortable being himself. His comfort made his audience comfortable.

Make it memorable

Why bother to speak if no one's going to remember what you said? And what are the keys to memorability? Relevant, well-delivered stories; anecdotes or examples about your own experience or people known by the audience; figures of speech (metaphors, similes). These techniques paint word pictures. They beat charts, graphs, numbers, and statistics. We may see or hear numbers, but we don't remember most of them. We certainly don't tell our family, friends, or colleagues about them, unless they deal with our pension.

Unfortunately, we don't think about memorability when we're called on to present. In fact, we've lost the art of the storyteller. Our culture and our role models seem to be demanding that we tell it with figures.

Microsoft PowerPoint has become a communication killer. It's a marvelous tool when used correctly. But most speakers have discovered it to be a great crutch. They use it as a manuscript and read along with what's on the screen. It's come to the point where I've seen speakers click a slide and say to the audience: "Now I realize you can't see what's on the screen, but...." Now there's a waste of my time. The year 2007 marked the 20th anniversary of the creation of PowerPoint. One of the creators said that it was a magnificent tool, but that most people used it badly. He compared it to the printing press, which improved written communication forever, but didn't prevent people from printing garbage. My rule: You should be your own best visual aid. That's the beauty of being a good teller of relevant and appropriate stories.

Speak from the heart

That's the art of saying what you mean and meaning what you say. It's getting involved with your subject matter. It's thinking about putting the audience first. When you stop thinking about yourself and start to concern yourself with getting the message across dynamically, you'll win the audience's gratitude and their attention. That's most easily accomplished when you personalize. Stories, anecdotes, and examples help you make it "from the heart."

A friend decided to run for office for the first time. He scheduled an announcement speech at a fund-raising dinner for friends, family, and potential donors. He asked me to help him with the delivery of his presentation. It was a typical political speech, written to impress the listeners with his competence, his qualifications, and understanding of the issues facing the voters. By the end of the second dull paragraph, I suggested he throw it away. We worked on telling the story of why he decided to run, what his neighbors told him they needed from government, and what his family was concerned about. On presentation night, as he approached the lectern, he brought out the original manuscript (many pages), threw them away, and said, "A friend told me this was garbage." Then he told them about why he was running and what they could expect from him. He spoke for less than five minutes and, as a vaudevillian does, he left his audience wanting more. I'm constantly watching politicians. And you know something? The best speeches candidates make are their concession speeches. Why? Because at last, they're speaking from the heart . No more acting. Just a replay of Bob Dole going back to being himself and speaking from the heart.

Keep it simple

My pseudo-mathematical formula is:

simple + brief + clear + concise = easy-to-understand.

I can't say it better than that. Think about how jarring it is to hear the police officer say: "We apprehended the alleged perpetrator exiting his vehicle in possession of a glasene container which housed a controlled substance." That's when a juror's eyes glaze over. Without realizing it, most of us are victims of this same disease: trying to impress rather than express. Make simplicity your rule for words, sentences, ideas, and whole speeches. Many politicians ignore this rule to their own detriment. They seem to believe that more is better; that quantity beats quality. I've hear very few speeches that I wish had lasted longer. Too many speakers feel an urgency to tell the audience everything they know. Well, no one wants to know everything you know. You need to learn and practice the art of verbal economy. Less is more. Simplicity goes hand-in-hand with being memorable. The easier you make it for me to understand your message, the more likely I am to remember it. Winston Churchill put the exclamation point on this subject: "Short words are the best. And short words, when old, are best of all."

Make it your own

One of my pet peeves is the person who takes a speech someone else writes and delivers it just that way—in someone else's words and style.

One of the keys to successful speaking is to deliver it your way; to make sure the words are words you'd use in normal conversation and not words that you or a speechwriter think are characteristic of a brilliant orator. William Safire writes the "On Language" column for the Sunday *New York Times*. He's a brilliant writer: articulate, literate, a language expert of the first order. But when he wrote speeches for others, he became a show-off and wound up making his clients look bad. It was Safire who gave Spiro Agnew, Nixon's vice president, the words describing the media as "nattering nabobs of negativism." The words were memorable, but in a bad way for Agnew, who obviously never would have used those words. Don't be tempted to write for the time capsule or for inclusion in a "Great Speeches" anthology. It won't work.

Edit yourself

The bottom line is this: Whether you write the speech yourself or someone else does it for you, ask yourself this question: *Would I use these words in these sentences on a normal day in a normal conversation with a friend?* If your answer is no, make sure you change it and bring it down to earth. As you write, I suggest you start with the premise that you're talking to a bright teenager. Then double-check it as you reread. An important thing to remember is to use contractions. Most of us say "don't, " "won't," and all the other apostrophe words. But in formal speaking we tend to use the two-word forms. That defeats our naturalness and tends to build a wall between the presenter and the audience. Contractions are the stuff of comfortable communication, so you should try to use them all the time. Think about this: A podium isn't a place for formal speech-making. It's a way to talk one-on-one to a group of people. There's nothing wrong with using words that will make the audience think—but if they *stop* and think, they'll miss the next thing you say.

The "Washington Word Game" in Chapter 7 is the classic example of speaking to impress. A good way to handle words that might be strange to some in the audience is to gracefully explain them: "I had an epiphany; the light bulb went on over my head." The easier our message is to absorb, the more impact we have. Unless you're an expert speaking to other experts in your field, use common, everyday words. Don't give your audience the chance to perceive you as a pompous ass.

Open strong

Those two words say it all. Get rid of "I'm delighted to be here today," "Let me begin by saying," "My dear friend, Dr. Whatzissname, asked me to be here today," "I'm flattered and humbled to have been invited to address this distinguished audience," or "I want to thank…." I call these openers "throat clearers." They're "a-hems." They do nothing but get you started without getting you started. In fact, they do just the opposite. They stop the audience cold and build a wall between the audience and your likability. One attempt to improve the impact of opening remarks was used so often that it became a cliché. Then it became a "groaner." I'm talking about the comics' "a funny thing happened to me on my way here." Audiences once upon a time looked forward to what came next. Not anymore. But you do need an opening with the impact that once had. Your objective is to make an instant connection with the audience. That brings us back to the relevant story, anecdote, example, word picture. When you open this way, you release yourself from the slavery of a text or PowerPoint presentation, and hooks the audience right away. Now they want to hear what comes next. Your opening should grab them.

Build the message, keep the focus, and make the point

In 1986, Governor Bill Clinton of Arkansas delivered the keynote address at the Democratic Nominating Convention. Clinton spoke. And he spoke. And he spoke. At the end of more than an hour of misery for the delegates and the world watching on television, he said, "in conclusion…." The auditorium erupted into an explosion of cheers and applause. They were thrilled that at last it would soon be over. I'm sure no one but the speechwriters have any idea of what he said. Fortunately for him, he learned from that experience, and he even used it to make fun of himself in future speeches. Unfortunately for us, very few other politicians learned from that. There was a time when long and super-long speeches were considered essential. Before radio and television, the main sources of news and entertainment were theatre, newspapers, and public speeches. That's why Edward Everett's two-hour oration at Gettysburgh got the rave reviews, whereas Lincoln's brilliant moment was considered to be short-changing the audience. The days of the old speech class maxim ("Tell them what you're going to tell them. Tell them. Then tell them what you've told them.") are gone. Or at least they should be. The important thing is to tell them what they need to know in a way they'll remember. Take another look at the O.J. Simpson trial comments in Chapter 2. It became a case of information overkill.

Close strong

Speakers rarely know how to end a speech. It' s so hard that most people—even professional speakers—end with "thank you." That's the equivalent of the Warner Brothers cartoon ending of "That's all, folks." It's a confession that there really is no strong ending, so "bye-bye." It's a weak way to leave the stage. Lately the world of speechmaking has added another exit line that now seems insincere. I'm talking about "God bless you and God Bless America." It's become a cliché. If you thank your audience, thank them for something important, such as coming to hear you in blizzard conditions. You might thank a sponsor who brought you. One way I've thanked sponsors who paid for my appearance at a not-for-profit association meeting is: "Anyone can give you a terrific shrimp cocktail and a great filet mignon. But tomorrow they're gone. If you feel you're taking something away you can use for the rest of your life, please thank the XYZ Company." Believe me: The sponsors love that message. Another strong ending is a memorable reminder of your message. I often close with the following Chinese proverb: "Tell me and I'll forget. Show me and I may remember. Involve me and I'll understand."

Selling Yourself in Confrontation and Media Interviews

It's amazing how confrontational we are.

Confrontation has become increasingly prevalent in communication. It often replaces civilized dialogue. People with opposing views start shouting, arguing, and going through the verbal equivalent of a fistfight. Unfortunately, there's no escape.

Every day we get to see the media practicing its version of "investigative journalism." We're constantly watching reporters play "gotcha" with politicians, business leaders, healthcare professionals, and clergy. No one is immune from the treatment. If you woke up this morning, you're fair game. In fact, not even the coffin excuses you from the treatment.

More and more, we're subjected to a right-leaning TV analyst facing off against a left-leaning colleague. They're really close friends, but arguments build ratings, so they yell and scream at each other for half an hour, then go out and enjoy dinner together.

The aura they create is that incivility is acceptable. Just as violence in film and television often inspires copycat acts, so, too, do tabloid television and hate radio.

The "Me" Syndrome

We watch otherwise-decent people behaving as though the world belongs to them. You've seen the person whose flight was cancelled screaming at the gate agent. Or the person at the checkout counter, yelling at the store clerk. Or the parent of the little-leaguer who thinks the coach made a colossal mistake and disapproves in an obnoxious way. The scenarios are endless and constant. And this doesn't even include road rage.

This selfish, rude, thoughtless, and inconsiderate "me first" mindset leads us right into imitating media role models. We structure our statements and questions exactly the way we've seen the tabloid interviewers do it. Without even being aware of it, we adopt what I call "the architecture of confrontation":

- A negative assumption.
- An accusation of wrongdoing.
- A buzzword or buzzwords.

A member of Congress showing off for television cameras in order to make the evening news doesn't ask the chemical company executive, "What actions are you taking to clean up the environment?" but rather, "Why are you poisoning our air and water?"

Accusations and Confrontation

Sound familiar? It should. It's what we're exposed to every day: people looking not for information, but trying to expose a scandal or trying to help someone else look bad. Sadly, many of us have picked up the technique.

Otherwise-decent people, mild-mannered folks, gentle souls become monsters in the public forum. More and more we're becoming a society of inquisitors and crucifiers rather than debaters and discussers. There was a time when civilized people could talk about sensitive subjects such as politics, religion, education, abortion, guns, and taxation. Now we're accusers, yellers, screamers, and arguers.

If you don't want confrontation, talk about the weather.

It's uncomfortable to be around confrontation, whether as a participant or an observer. When two people are shouting at each other, seemingly refusing to hear (or, I should say, listen to) the other point of view, we're embarrassed. This is true even if one of the screamers is representing a view we share.

We've become so used to the offensive technique of the loaded question that we use it ourselves. More often then not, we don't even realize we're doing exactly what we dislike when others do it.

Everyday situations become confrontational, as we're intimidated by the reporter, the attorney, the public official, the colleague, the neighbor, and, worst of all, the family member. The end result is that we dread being involved in any situation that may evolve into a confrontation. It doesn't have to be that way. We don't have to get angry, defensive, shout back, and fall apart.

The Confrontation Bomb

I remember my first Parent Teacher Association experience. The school board had just closed a school in town. We'll call it "School #3." At the meeting to announce the closing, the first question came from a neighbor of mine. He was a very pleasant person, but closing his neighborhood school was a real personal affront. His question should have been, "Why did you close School #3?"

Instead, using the architecture of confrontation, he shouted, "Why are you ruining our schools?" The untrained board chairman yelled back, "We're not ruining the schools." So began the shouting match. It was a true "lose-lose" situation.

Defusing Confrontation

I started out in this area of communication training at the U.S. Chamber of Commerce, helping business and association executives become aware of the techniques used by the reporter whose goal was to *make* a story rather than report one. I focused on the communication skills that would help them beat the reporters at their own game. Then I realized that the same techniques could be used to defuse all public demonstrations of arrogance, rudeness, intimidation, confrontation, and heckling. I studied the methods used by reporters and confronters, and the techniques that could defeat them. Those techniques are easy to learn, and you can use them anytime someone wants to make you look bad.

How People Respond to You

First, let's review some key points from Chapter 1.

There are four ways people can judge you when they're seeing you for the first time:

- They can like you.
- They can dislike you.
- They can be neutral to you (not leaning one way or the other).
- They can feel sorry for you.

Your goal should be to communicate to the audience, not to the confronter; the best way to accomplish that is to be liked.

Second, almost always, there are three points of view represented in an audience when the subject is controversial, volatile, and emotional.

Some of the people already share your point of view. Forget them.

Some have already made up their minds on the other side of the issue. Forget them.

Remember: The object of your communication should always be the people whose minds are not yet made up.

They haven't decided.

That's how elections are won.

It's how court cases are decided.

I don't have to tell you that one undecided juror can control the outcome of the trial.

In the Bush-Gore election, a few thousand wavering voters could have changed the outcome.

Take the abortion issue, for example. No one fervently debating the issue, whether brilliant or terrible, is going to change another person's point of view on one of the most divisive subjects of our time. The winner of that debate will be the person who most appeals to the undecided in the audience. The good debater can't possibly win over the people of the other side. The awful debater can't possibly lose the people who share his or her ideology. So your goal is always to be liked by the uncommitted.

That's the objective, and it establishes a brand-new set of ground rules in a confrontational situation. These new rules are:

- Pause. Think before you speak.

- Stay calm and reasonable.

- Don't get angry. Keep control of your temper.

- Refuse to take the attack personally.

- Be positive.

- Give information rather than denials.

- Be explanatory. Don't succumb to the temptation to argue.

- Take lots of time. Let your opponent rush, shout, run off at the mouth, argue, yell, and scream. By taking your time, you'll infuriate him or her even further and make your opponent appear irrational to the audience you're trying to win.

- Be the voice of reason.

- Be the good guy, Mr. or Ms. Nice.

- Make intellectual love to your audience.

How Do You Do *All* This?

I can hear you saying, "That's easy for you to say." Well, there are certain techniques that I've found that really work. You've learned how important it is to please the audience with your face, your body, and your voice. But even if you're doing everything right, there may be some members of your audience you cannot please. Obviously, the hostile questions or the confrontational remarks are not going to come from your supporters. Those who have not yet made up their minds will usually remain silent. So, you have to learn how to handle your adversaries. And here are the techniques you can use to do that.

Remember to Pause

The most important technique is the pause. It's also the hardest to accomplish in taking control of what might otherwise be an uncontrollable situation.

We naturally react and want to react quickly—don't. It's unnatural to stop and think before we speak. In fact, it's so unnatural that we've developed a whole vocabulary of spoken pauses—audible pauses—pauses filled with the strange extraneous sounds I talked about in some detail in Chapter 2:

- "Uh."
- "Ya know."
- "Like."
- "And so."
- "Know what I mean?"

Sometimes we use garbage fillers, phrases, and sentences. I'm tired of "so to speak," "if you will," "as it were," "at this point in time," and "in a manner of speaking." John F. Kennedy had "let me say this about that." Richard M. Nixon's classic was "let me make one thing perfectly clear." Some others we hear all the time are:

- "I'm glad you asked me that question."
- "To be perfectly honest (or frank)."
- "To tell you the truth." (Have you been lying so far?)

You can probably add several more, but you get the idea. They're spoken attempts to get the mind in gear. Instead, stop and think.

- Don't move your mouth until your mind is in "Drive."

- Don't start in "Park."

- Don't start in "Reverse."

- Don't start in "Neutral."

Wait until you're ready to move forward.

It's difficult; it's even unnatural. But it's an essential first step. It avoids the disastrous pitfall:

- Ready.

- *Fire.*

- Aim.

The "ah..." person who makes "uh..." sounds while "er..." talking seems unsure, uncertain of where he or she is going, insecure, and not used to thinking on his feet. The silent pause helps your audience create a more positive image of you. It also throws your adversary off balance. Did you hear the question? How are you going to reply to the hostile remark? And while your adversary is wondering, you're thinking, framing your reply. You are in control of the situation, not your adversary.

Maintain Eye Contact

The second thing to do as you pause is maintain eye contact with the person who's being aggressive, confrontational, intimidating, or obnoxious. That doesn't mean staring directly into this person's eyes. It means finding a comfortable place on his or her face and keeping your eyes there. Don't let your eyes wander.

As with the audible pause, eye movement tends to make an audience think "dishonest," "shifty-eyed," "untrustworthy," and "looking for a way out of a bad situation." But if you look directly at your adversary, you will give the impression of being honest, thoughtful, reasonable, and trustworthy. And once again, your adversary is thrown off balance, wondering what's coming next. He won't know where to look.

You are in control.

The Considered Response

I call the pause the digestive of the mind. It will give you valuable time to frame your answer to a hostile or loaded question. As you do so, first eliminate the negative, the accusations, and the buzzwords from the questions. By all means, answer the question, and answer honestly. That's most important. But don't give the questioner what he or she is looking for—don't repeat buzzwords.

Don't deny accusations. Don't tell him he's wrong or that he has his facts mixed up.

Even though we do these things quite naturally, believe it or not, they're wrong. They're wrong from the perspective of winning the audience. Use the pause *to translate the question into what it would have been if it had been asked by a decent human being.* That will help you answer from your perspective.

For example:

- **"Why are you killing and maiming?"**
  Becomes: "Tell me about your company's safety record."

- **"Why are you ripping off the customer?"**
  Becomes: "Tell me about your pricing policy."

- **"Why are you cheating our kids out of a decent education?"**
  Becomes: "Tell me about the progress the schools are making."

- **"Why are you promoting a risky tax scheme?"**
  Becomes: "What does your tax plan do for me?"

Never, never!

Obviously, the untrained will answer:

- **"We're not killing and maiming."**
- **"We're not ripping off the customer."**
- **"We're not cheating the kids."**
- **"It's not a risky tax scheme."**

Don't be caught in the trap

The confronter has planted a weed. Your job is to pull out the weed by the roots. But the wrong answer, one that repeats the buzzword and denies the accusation, waters the weed.

At my first training program for the American Library Association, I asked a competent young library director, "Why do you distribute smut?" She was startled and asked, "Smut?" I snarled, "Smut!" She replied, "We don't distribute smut." Many of the librarians in the audience came up to me afterward and said, "You're absolutely right. All I could remember from your time with her was 'smut.'"

The Lethal Buzzword

The power of the buzzword was never more aptly demonstrated to me than one night while watching a tabloid TV show. It was one of the many stepchildren of *60 Minutes.* The segment I saw was titled "Killer Trucks." The script never used the word *truck* without the antecedent *killer.* So, I heard *killer trucks* over and over again. As they came to the end of the segment, the voice-over went silent. On came a series of fast-cut photos of trucks that had demolished other wheeled vehicles: baby carriages, tricycles, wagons, bicycles, motorcycles, cars, vans, SUVs, other trucks. The soundtrack was a quiet country musician with guitar accompaniment singing:

> *There's a killer on the road.*
> *There's a killer on the road.*
> *There's a killer, killer, killer, killer, killer, killer, killer.*
> *There's a killer on the road.*

The screen went blank. Silence. Episode over.

I'm reluctant to admit it, but the next time I was driving on the interstate and looked in my rearview mirror and saw an 18-wheeler coming up fast behind me, I broke into a cold sweat.

I'm convinced that the outcome of the 2004 election was tipped by the buzzword *flip-flop*. We heard it endlessly. Then it was reinforced by visuals showing John Kerry windsurfing, first in one direction and then the other. It was so powerful that it was used against every candidate in the '08 race, and I'll bet it becomes a staple in all future campaigns: national, state, and local.

That's the power of the buzzword.

Give Valuable Information

To connect with an audience and get your message across, your information must be honest, positive, and caring.

Honest

If you make it a practice to tell the truth, to avoid exaggerating or guessing (remember Al Gore "inventing the Internet" and a half-dozen other questionable achievements?), you never have to issue corrections, apologies, or retractions, and you never have to remember what you said.

Bill Clinton is an excellent communicator, but his entire administration was hindered and nearly brought down by his seeming inability to confront the truth. I'm convinced that if he hadn't been so likable, the impeachment proceedings would have gone against him. Think about this scenario: America watched him on television. He said "I did not have sexual relations with that woman." And the public responded: "You liar!!!...I like you."

If you don't know the answer to a question, say so. But then volunteer to get the information and get back.

If you don't understand the question, say so.

If there's a problem, acknowledge it, and then tell us what you're going to do about it.

Positive

Speakers and political candidates who bad-mouth the opposition (in politics) or the competition (in sales) increasingly turn off audiences. If you're the best, you shouldn't need to put anyone else down. It's hard to hear an accusation and not deny it, but a "what I do" is much stronger than "I don't." Try to eliminate the words *do not* from you vocabulary.

It works!

In my training session with the president of Volvo North America, when I got to explaining how to "translate the question into what it would have been if it were asked by a decent human being," he responded enthusiastically, "Arch, you've just taught me how to play a new game. If this were tennis, I could beat McEnroe." I loved that image. I'd never thought of my training as a game, and realized that if I can help you improve on a game you enjoy, the learning process would be greatly simplified and improved for you.

Here's what happened to him:

A few weeks later he accepted an invitation to appear on the *Today Show*. The interviewer did the "gotcha" bit. She said, "Everyone knows the automobile that's manufactured today is piece of junk. Why are you involved in the manufacture and sale of junk?"

He called me when the show went off the air and chuckled. He said, "Three weeks ago, I would have angrily said, 'The Volvo is not junk.'" With 8 to 12 million people watching, he said, "I'm proud to be able to tell you that the average life of a Volvo on the highway in Sweden has reached 19 and a half years. Imagine driving the car you're driving today for almost 20 years. And I'm even prouder of the fact that Volvo has become the standard of safety for the entire automotive industry."

He sold cars. I believe he sold more cars than he'd have sold if Volvo had bought a dozen commercials during the Super Bowl.

Caring

No one succeeds the way a loving communicator does. It's as essential an element as breathing. When you care about me, I care back. So here are a few spoken lead-ins that will serve two purposes in confrontation and media interviews: They'll help you occasionally limit the silent pauses, and they'll give your statement a caring opening.

- "I'm sorry you feel that way...."
- "I understand how you could reach that conclusion...."
- "Let me explain what the facts really are...."
- "If I understood your question, what you're really asking me is...."
- "I'm proud to be able to tell you...."

Caution. Don't repeat any of them in a given exchange or you'll sound programmed. If they're not comfortable for you, stay with the silent pause with constant eye contact. We always feel that the person who repeats the same lead-in over and over again seems automated and is the victim of bad coaching.

Bill Clinton was very effective in a debate when he walked to the edge of the stage and said, "I feel your pain." That gesture was hugely successful for him, but then he made the mistake of repeating it several times in subsequent public appearances. The repetition destroyed whatever statement followed.

In vice-presidential debates during the 2000 election, I stopped counting how many times Dick Cheney said, "Governor Bush and I..." and Joe Lieberman said, "Al Gore and I...." Someone must have said to each, "Look, you're running for #2 on the ticket. Don't let them forget who's #1."

And don't forget: With caring, the silent pause with warm, glowing eye contact works every time.

Simple, Brief, Clear, Concise, and Easy-to-Understand

I spoke about telling your audience only what it needs to know for you to get your message. The overwhelming instinct to appear professional has caused many people to develop "losing" speaking habits. Our role models lead us into the trap of believing that being pompous pays.

Words Meant to Impress That Don't

We've littered our language with garbage words. Some that come to mind right away are:

- Paradigm.

- Infrastructure.

- All the "-ize" words, such as utilize, prioritize, maximize, optimize.

- Concomitant.

- Concupiscence.

- Acronyms understood only by your profession.

- Plethora.

- Extrapolate.

- Internecine.

- Penultimate.

- Erstwhile.

They're all part of the misunderstanding that makes people believe they must impress an audience rather than express themselves.

Then–CIA director George Tenet negotiated a tricky cease-fire in the Middle East in June 2001.

One member of the negotiating team, General Eiland, attributed the success of the mission this way: "Tenet said the clearest possible things and used simple, clear words."

Listen to Winston Churchill again: "Short words are the best, and short words, when old, are best of all."

When we're trying to figure out what you mean, we're missing your next thought. Don't try to tell us everything you know. We don't want to know everything you know.

The Washington word game

This game pops up from time to time in newspapers and magazines and makes my point for me.

You're to select one word from each of the three columns and put together a perfectly governmentese phrase. The more words you use, the less likely you are to say anything meaningful while still managing to sound important. Try any combination of one word from each column.

The Washington Word Game		
Column A	**Column B**	**Column C**
indigenous	environmental	overkill
comprehensive	neutral	pollution
fragmentary	concomitant	interface
interplanetary	philosophical	replication
internecine	totalitarian	exacerbation
collective	demagogic	dialectic
bureaucratic	proactive	evaluation
portentous	demonstrative	resonance
didactic	hedonistic	fallacy
pedantic	antediluvian	methodology
penultimate	gustatory	phalanx
incorrigible	retrogressive	dyslexia
corporeal	pragmatic	monasticism

Memorable

The key is getting your message across in such an effective way that your audience will remember it.

You can be memorable in a good way or a bad way.

Guess which one I recommend.

Disastrously memorable

I was in the audience at a breakfast meeting at the U.S. Chamber of Commerce. The audience was made up of business leaders, lobbyists, association executives, legislators, and professionals in every field. The featured speaker was then–Secretary of the Interior James Watt. In the middle of his talk, he put on an impish grin and said (I don't remember the exact words, but it was something along these lines): "We have the perfect coalition. We have a woman, a black, two Jews, and a cripple." He got a huge laugh but lost his job.

It was memorable, all right. Unfortunately so.

People are still quoting it years later.

Making a connection

Earlier I said, "Tell them what they want to know." That means that to be memorable, you have to connect with them. The best way to do that is to tell stories. Use anecdotes and personal examples; paint word pictures using similes and metaphors.

"What have you done for me lately?" will often be one of the questions you should answer. How will you affect my income, my future, and my family?

Tell stories

Notice that I said stories, mind you, not jokes. Not smart-aleck comedy. And remember: Buzzwords are memorable. You have to be more memorable in your responses than the buzzword that was used against you.

As with the other aspects of this training, the memorable answer isn't easy to come by. But awareness of the concept and its importance will help you develop a technique and incorporate it into your style.

Learn by practicing

Our role models have led us to believe that an audience is most impressed by generalities, statistics, charts, graphs, numbers, big words, and pompous pronouncements. They are wrong. Memorability, as can the silent pause and eye contact, can be practiced. Anywhere. With anyone.

You can even practice by watching TV interviews and paying attention to the answers. See if you can produce a memorable response. What would you have done to make a dull answer come alive?

A few years back, a man was arrested for conducting what he called "eating tours" in a large metropolitan park. For a small fee, he walked people through the park, cutting samples of edible and nourishing plants that grew wild in the park and letting the tour group taste them.

The park police picked him up. He was booked and jailed on the charge of defacing the park.

A TV reporter saw this on the police blotter and decided to make mincemeat out of the parks commissioner. He grabbed a camera crew and raced down to city hall. He caught the parks commissioner as he was leaving his office.

"Commissioner," he said, camera rolling, "operating in your park at this very moment are pimps, prostitutes, cocaine dealers, crack dealers, heroin dealers—the dregs of society. Yet, your park police have just arrested a man for making an honest living in the park. Sir, what kind of thinking is this?"

The parks commissioner thought for a moment, smiled, and said, "What you don't understand is he's not eating *in* the park; he's *eating the park.*"

Notice the question. There was crime in the park. The police knew it and worried about it. The reporter's question spoke to that concern. The question was loaded with truth, but it was loaded. It would have been natural for the commissioner to get defensive about the problem. Instead, he cut through the garbage in that loaded question and was able to ask himself what the real question was. He realized that he was asked, "Why did you allow the man to be arrested?" And that's the question he answered.

Some *interesting* examples

In the first presidential debate of the 2000 election, George Bush threw a zinger at Al Gore. He called Gore's plan "fuzzy math." Similar to "I feel your pain," it was wonderfully effective the first time, but he repeated it many times in that same debate and it lost its edge.

Al Gore came back with, "His plan will only benefit the wealthiest 1 percent of Americans." He repeated it ad nauseum. It wasn't even a strong example because the imagery was vague. No one *saw* the wealthiest 1 percent.

I'm convinced that had Bill Clinton been the debate opponent, he'd have smiled and said, "Dick Cheney got a $60-million golden parachute from Halliburton, the oil giant. He'll get millions more from your tax breaks. That's money you're stealing from the classroom."

The audience would respond to that kind of word picture.

One memorable image

I was scheduled to do a training program on a Sunday morning for the Leadership Conference of the National School Boards Association. There was a Saturday session they called a "Congress," and I attended it to learn about the current issues of concern to school board members.

The topic was standardized testing. Everyone attending was allowed a few minutes to deliver a prepared statement on the subject. As with any other controversial subject, there were people in the room strongly for testing. There were people ardently against it. And there was a large group that hadn't made up its mind.

Lots of folks got up, buried their noses into the lectern, and read—or rather droned—on and on. It was naptime. No one scored many points for or against testing.

Finally, the chair recognized one man. He walked to the lectern, took a long pause as his eyes surveyed the room, and said, "Folks, you can't fatten a hog by weighing it." He nodded, waited for a reaction to set in, then walked back to his seat, and sat down.

A few people started chuckling right away. Then others realized what had just been said.

Before long the place was rocking. They cheered. Even people on the other side of the issue were applauding him for his memorability.

In fact, I was able to use that moment in my training program the next day. I asked, "What do you remember from yesterday?" I could have conducted the response as if they were a glee club: "You can't fatten a hog by weighing it." I'm certain it was the subject of conversation long after the meeting ended.

Why? Because it was:

- Simple.

- Brief.

- Easy to understand.

- Memorable.

And it said it all.

Don't Succumb to Sound Bites

Each of the examples so far can be called a "sound bite."

Sound bites are very short and quotable statements.

I believe that the press has become hungry for sound bites because most people have lost the art of the storyteller. Nothing works as well as relevant stories told well. When you put an answer in story form, humanize it, and personalize it, people stop, pay attention, and remember. In fact, storytelling has slowly worked its way into print journalism. In the old days, journalism school insisted that the opening paragraph of a story should answer the questions *who*, *what*, *where*, *when*, and *why*. Now it's "Hook them in the first paragraph with a story opening."

Here are a few first lines of *New York Times* news stories I found on a single day:

"Dick Richards was pounding the drums and thinking of the girls on the beach."

"It was a routine action that makes any officer vulnerable: Two police officers stopped a car in Brooklyn and were shot and wounded—one so gravely that he was on life support."

"With their teacher absent, 10 students were allowed to leave school early."

"Few actions police officers take are as routine—or deadly—as stopping a car."

"In the biggest organized crime trial here in years, jurors scribbled dutifully in notebooks Monday as the son of a reputed mob leader offered a rare, almost surreal how-to lesson about growing up in the 'Chicago Outfit.'"

"Inside a drab cellphone shop, set deep inside the sprawling Baqaa refugee camp on the outskirts of this city Muhammed Khalil and his friends were as gloomy as the fluorescent lights that flickered on the ceiling."

"For some couples in the Bronx lately, it has been easy to fall in love, but hard to get married."

You can't go wrong if the elements of a story are in your statement. Even television news shows will make the time for a really well-told story when it advances the news item.

Don't feel compelled to answer in five or seven seconds. The sound bite is an artificial device to make up for the fact that most of us have succumbed to being dull, uninteresting, and pompous.

When rare political figures who speak memorably and colorfully come along, they dominate the news. Anecdotes; figures of speech, both similes and metaphors; personal examples from your experience or the questioner's experience; and quotations that fit perfectly all have the impact of the great story, but they have to be well told and they must be relevant.

I've encouraged many clients to create a story exchange within the organization. Most of us have great stories of accomplishment, but we're either afraid that we'll sound boastful or we've simply forgotten how much impact stories can have.

Unfortunately, most adults have lost the art of storytelling. We've become so busy making ends meet that we've simply gone stale with stories.

Single-parent families and two-working-parent families don't realize that they're shortchanging their kids by failing to put stories into the youngsters' lives. The bottom line is that children don't get their imaginations tickled, and adults forget how to tell a good story effectively.

The impact of a good story

Let me share one experience I had. I did a training program for a joint meeting of the South Carolina School Boards and Administrators. Everyone in the audience was a board member, a superintendent, a principal, or an assistant of one. I spent a lot of time on storytelling. I even had the audience members share stories that they felt were strong statements about the effectiveness of the school, success stories that they never would have thought of using to answer questions about the "failure" of public schools.

After the program I was driven to the airport by one of the superintendents. The following is what he shared with me:

"Arch, never stop encouraging adults to use stories. They really work. Today's children have been put in front of a television set. Their imaginations have been ossified. Some of them have *never had a story told to them.* My wife is a kindergarten teacher. Most of the 5-year-olds have never heard a good story told well, so she's banished television from her classroom and teaches in story form.

"To get the children used to learning from stories, she spends the first couple of school days telling the classic stories. This year she sat on the floor and assembled the children in four semicircular rows around her with a small aisle in the middle.

"She opened the school year with, 'Once upon a time there was a girl named Red Riding Hood.' As she spoke, she looked around the room. All the faces in the room were registering, 'What is this garbage?...What's going on here?' Then she got to Grandma and there was a glimmer of recognition. And when she said, '*big bad wolf,*' they understood the danger.

"One little boy got really caught up and wiggled his way from the back to the front as she wound up with, 'And the wolf *ate up* Grandma.'

"That little 5-year-old, eyes big as saucers, looked up at her and said, 'That son of a bitch.'"

Stories work. They provide an immediate connection between you and your audience.

Pride Doesn't Mean Arrogance

Most of us grew up with parents and loved ones who constantly told us, "Don't brag." "Don't be boastful." "Don't go around blowing your own horn." And so we feel very uncomfortable calling attention to things we've done that we're proud of.

What we fail to realize is that there can be a tremendous difference between blowing your own horn and telling an audience about things you're proud of having been a part of.

Style and attitude make the difference

Much of the difference is in the style and attitude involved in the telling. It's basically the difference between the colossal ego and the person who's genuinely humble but proud of having done really good work. The colossal ego comes on as "Mighty Mouth." The words *I* and *me* dominate the communication. What people hear is: "You couldn't have done it without me. I'm personally responsible for this triumph." It's so much more pleasant to hear, "I'm proud to be part of this terrific team." Think about it. It's one of the fine lines in all interpersonal communication.

A simple, honest self-appraisal is best

Resume-writing and job interviews are akin to walking a tightrope: How do I make myself seem to be the best possible applicant for the job without making myself appear to be the most egotistical oaf in the world? And remember: Almost every communication can be likened to a job interview, making a sale, campaigning for elective office, or making a presentation.

The style and attitude of your pride in yourself, your product, or your idea are the keys to the audience's appreciation of you as a trustworthy, competent, and likable person. Statements such as "I'm the greatest" can't work. But no one will object to "I love what I do. I do it well. And I'm always looking for ways to do it better."

Here are a few samples of the kind of statements that could be preceded by, "I'm proud to tell you," but don't need those words spoken because the sentiment is implied.

- "One client (customer) thanked me the other day for...."

- "A resident called to tell me that her life was changed by...."

- "Several patients said their condition was dramatically improved after...."

- "We've been in business for more than X years, and a lot of our original customers are still coming here for...."

- "Members are constantly thanking our staff for...."

There's got to be a way to tell other people about things you've done that you're proud of without turning them off or turning them against you.

Find it.

More About Media Interviews

You may be interviewed for any number of reasons, such as:

- You're an expert in your field.

- Your company researchers have just made a wonderful discovery.

- You were an eyewitness to something newsworthy.

- Your neighbor won the lottery.

- Your colleague was just arrested.

- You support or oppose a controversial move by the city council, the zoning board, or the school board.

- You were the victim of a consumer scam.

- You're running for office.

- You just happen to "be there" when someone needs an interviewee.

It's truly an endless list, and depending on the reason and the medium (newspaper, magazine, radio, TV), the choice of site may be obvious. If the reporter is from a newspaper or magazine, the interview will usually be in your office, your home, a restaurant, or the publication's office.

Print Interviews

A print interview may be the most comfortable for you because the environment seems relaxed. It will almost always be conducted sitting down. After all, the interviewer will be taking notes.

Radio interviews will usually be conducted at the station's studio or over the phone.

Each involves two people: the interviewer and the interviewee. It can be "live" (aired at the time you're speaking) or taped—and possibly edited—to be aired later.

Whether it's print or live, if you have advance knowledge that it's going to happen, I urge you to have a small tape recorder running for your own personal record of what you said.

Television Interviews

Television offers almost limitless options concerning site. If a camera, a microphone, and a reporter can get there, the interview can happen. The most common situations are:

- In a studio.

- On the street.

- In or outside your office.

- At an event.

- At the scene of a breaking story.

It's not as casual as it seems.

Most of us are more comfortable on our own turf (our home or office), but let me remind you that once you factor in all the equipment and personnel that go into a video interview, there's no such thing as "home turf" for you. You're just not used to cameras, lights, recorders, cables, and a bunch of people speaking a foreign language—in this case, "video-ese." You have no idea how disruptive it can be because the at-home interview looks so intimate and unobtrusive to the viewer.

It's not uncommon for the crew to leave behind a mountain of food and beverage containers, or to have rearranged furniture that never makes it back into place.

And to add insult to injury, the phone and utility bills could pay for a shuttle launch.

The Advantage of the Studio Interview

The studio is a good site. The lighting is most likely professional and favorable. There's usually a make-up person to help you look your best for television. The interview has probably been planned, so you may know the subject and have an opportunity to prepare. All these are factors in your favor.

The studio interview will either be one on one or else you'll appear as one of the guests. Normally, there won't be a studio audience. Not so, of course, on the syndicated talk shows, but those dynamics take care of themselves when you learn all the techniques of giving a good interview.

A stand-up interview in a studio is rare. You may be asked to make an entrance or an exit, but you'll probably always be sitting for the actual interview. So, in your home, in your office, or in a studio, you'll almost certainly be sitting. Most of us are more comfortable, more at ease, in a chair. But beware. Our posture training doesn't always cover sitting, and no two chairs are alike. The secret is to be able to look comfortable without slouching. If you're given a swivel chair, don't fall into the trap of moving from side to side or rocking back and forth. Rhythmic movement is monotonous, hypnotic, and sleep-inducing.

Sitting technique

Keep your knees together. Television technicians call spread knees "the crotch shot." You can put your knees together and your heels together, or cross your ankles. As I mentioned in Chapter 5, if you cross your legs, angle the top leg down. The camera should never see the sole of your shoe. It's the ugliest part of your clothing, and the camera will invariably find the gum (or worse) you stepped in on the way to the studio.

Know where to look

One of the questions I'm asked most often is, "Where do I look? Should I look at the interviewer or the camera?" You'll never go wrong if you look at the person you're talking to. My recommendation is never look at the camera unless the host says something such as, "What would you tell our audience watching at home?" Begin your answer looking at the person who asked the question, and then gracefully glide toward the camera. But if you do that, be certain you know which camera to look at. One of the worst moments on TV news is when the reporter is looking at the wrong camera.

The same principle applies to the telephone caller. If you're part of a call-in show, the producer, director, or stage manager will probably brief you before airtime. If no one tells you which camera represents the caller, *ask.* If you're one of a group, as in a panel, make it a point to look at the moderator or another panelist—preferably the person who's speaking. When it's your turn, or if you interject, be sure to look at the person you're talking to, answering, or interrupting.

When some other panelist is hogging airtime, don't fall into the trap of a shouting match. Only a political junkie enjoys the yelling-interrupting-talking-over-one-another school of high-pitched, shrill, "I know better than you" TV performing. If you're surrounded by these types, occasionally interject a good-natured comment such as, "Hello there. Remember me?" or "How about another point of view?" An intelligent audience will wonder why the rude ones are ignoring you and may even wonder if the others aren't actually afraid of hearing what you have to say. I really like it when the speaker responds to the professional interrupter with, "Let me finish, Joe," or "Joe, you had your turn. Now let me have mine."

When the show includes a studio audience, you have to be even more careful. The cameras have been arranged to shoot you from the perspective of the person who's talking to you. So, your job is to look at the host, the audience, or the other panelist, whoever is talking, or the one who invited you to speak. It's an excellent rule.

Most of these ground rules apply when an interview is scheduled for your office. If the crew includes a make-up person, let that person make you up. If not, you should get a quick lesson in make-up before the crew is scheduled to arrive and put on the simplest application.

The Stand-Up Interview

For most of us, the toughest interview to handle is the stand-up interview. People are not at their best standing up on the street, at an event, or at a function. These are tough because they're almost always spontaneous. You'll probably be surprised, maybe even shocked. You may not be able to disguise the fact that you weren't expecting this. You haven't prepared yourself physically or psychologically for the interview. You're just as likely to be thinking, "Is my hair mussed?" or "Do I look okay?" as "How can I get my best point across?"

Of course, if you're standing around a crime scene, an accident site, or on the courthouse steps during a controversial trial, you should expect nothing less than having a microphone shoved in your face and a question shouted at you. There'll be camera crews galore, and if one camera gets pointed at you, all the other reporters will flock to you, thinking the other station has just found an "expert."

There you are with microphones pointed at you from all directions.

Several reporters are now shouting questions simultaneously and all the while demonstrators are chanting their rehearsed slogans.

People are pushing you.

Sirens are blaring.

Horns are honking and the egomaniacs are crowding you out to wave at the camera.

The sun is shining right in your eyes. Or, if it's dark, the TV lights are. Maybe the weather is rotten, and you're in physical discomfort.

The biggest mistake you can make is to assume that you'll do okay because you know what you're talking about. A lot of otherwise-bright folks have been led like lambs to the slaughter because they felt they could open their mouths and the information would undoubtedly come out right.

Time and again, I'm amazed by the lack of smarts graphically demonstrated by public officials, doctors, business executives, contractors, attorneys, and other intelligent professionals who agree to appear on television without specific, specialized training. You'd think they'd have figured out by now that intimidation, controversy, and confrontation are what keep TV interview shows on the air.

My final word on the interview site is this: No matter where you're interviewed, you're not likely to feel completely comfortable. That's why you're unlikely to look, sound, and act natural until you *learn* to do just that, even under the stressful conditions of being confronted by a reporter with pad, microphone, or camera.

Winning Interviews

Here are some pointers for giving a winning interview. All the concepts are easy to understand, and they're not easy to do, but they're universals.

◨ **Prepare:** As soon as a group of you understands the skills, rehearse. Throw the toughest curveballs you can at one another and practice, practice, practice. Then you'll know what you want to say and how to say it.

◨ **Pause:** Stop and think before you speak. A second or two seems eternal to the untrained speaker, but the audience really welcomes a chance to think about what's just been said.

◼ **Remain silent:** Keep quiet in the uh...um...ya know...pause. Know what I mean? In the practice sessions, hit the table each time you hear an extraneous sound. Pretty soon they'll begin to disappear.

◼ **Maintain eye contact:** No one has trust in your competence or can like you without qualification if your eyes are all over the place instead of on your audience as you speak.

◼ **Inform:** Don't take the trouble to say anything if you have nothing to say. As a corollary, don't speak "off the record." If you don't want to see it in print, hear it on the radio, or watch it repeated on television, *don't say it*.

◼ **Be honest:** Be willing to acknowledge a problem's existence. Be willing to admit you don't have all the answers.

◼ **Be positive:** Don't use the words *don't* or *won't*. Tell us what is. Tell us what will be.

◼ **Be simple:** Get rid of jargon. Stop delivering literature and deliver conversation.

◼ **Be memorable:** Use stories, anecdotes, examples, similes, and metaphors. Personalize. Bring the audience *into* your message. Paint word pictures.

◼ **Be proud:** You or your team has accomplished something memorable; share it. Don't hide it.

◼ **Smile:** Show me you like me.

◼ **Open your face:** Show me you care.

◼ **Gesture:** Hug me from a distance.

◼ **Finally:** Don't get angry. Don't lose your cool. Don't take an attack personally. That's playing right into the hands of the tabloid reporter. It makes good copy for everyone but *you*. Be the voice of reason.

Win the game.

Don't deny—*educate*.

Don't negate—*inform*.

Don't fall into the buzzword trap—*tell a story that relevantly contradicts the error.*

Interview Traps

The well-trained interviewee looks at the media as the other team in a game. Just as in any other game, there are strategies involved. Taken to an extreme, you could call it a war. The idea is to win or, at worst, to play to a draw. The media uses certain traps or land mines. Here's what to look for:

1. Architecture

The first, foremost, and premier tactic involves the loaded question. It's built on negatives, accusations, and buzzwords. Those are the building blocks. This is the trap I covered at length earlier ("Why are you part of a rip-off?" "Why are you contributing to the poisoning of the environment?"). Reduced to its lowest common denominator, your job is to eliminate these elements from your answer. Don't deny the accusation; avoid the negative. Don't repeat the buzzwords. The intent here is to put you on the defensive rather than to solicit information. And your job is to give information.

2. Rhythm

There are reporters who've developed a style borrowed from some trial lawyers. First, they establish a rapport through a series of very simple, basic questions that establish the belief that this is going to be a no-brainer. Then, when you've picked up their rhythm, along comes the zinger.

- "State your full name." Fast answer.
- "Where do you live?" Fast answer.
- "How long have you lived there?" Fast answer.
- "Are you married?" Fast answer.
- "Where do you work?" Fast answer.

- "How long have you worked there?" Fast answer.
- "Why do you overcharge?" POW!

That's how the rhythm trap works. When you force yourself to pause for a split second even before you give your name, the adversary soon senses that you're on to the game. In a legal proceeding, the pause gives your attorney a chance to object before you've blurted out an answer, and in this training the pause lets your mind act as its own attorney, "object," and work out a good response.

3. The Double-Edged Sword

This is the two-pronged question designed to help you make an ass of yourself in public.

- "Was this a case of stupidity or insensitivity?"
- "Which candidate will do the most damage?"

Again, the intention is to prevent you from riding between the horns of a dilemma without a saddle. Here, the only recourse is to pause and reshape the question into what it would have been if the adversary had played fair.

In the first case, the question might have been, "What happened?" So, "Let me explain what happened" is a perfectly legitimate beginning.

In the second question, a simultaneous translation into decency would ask, "How do you size up the candidates?" A beginning such as, "Each candidate has strengths and weaknesses, just like any other human being" will lead you away from instantaneous disaster and an inadvertent step onto the land mine.

4. Prolonged Silence

A lot of reporters will leave the microphone pointed at your face after you've finished. They'll intentionally delay bringing the microphone back to themselves. For you, it becomes a long, agonizing pause. The key is: Don't say another word. Once you've finished, *stop*. A prolonged silence won't make it on the air unless you "cooperate" by falling apart. Remember: You're simply being invited to say something you'll regret, in the stress of the silence. If the pause seems to be getting absurdly long, you only have to smile and say, "Did you have another question?" or "Was there something else you wanted to talk about?" or "Didn't you understand what I said?" The audience is bright enough to know that you've answered the original question. Your job is to call attention to the fact that you're refusing the obvious invitation to put your foot in your mouth. Quite often, it's what's said after you've finished that causes all the trouble.

5. Persistence

More and more we're being victimized by reporters asking the same question, or a slightly different version of the same question, endlessly. The design here is to exasperate you, to get you to the point where you're so frustrated that you blurt out something you later wish you'd never said. And, of course, that's the response that makes it into the story or on the air. The intention is to get you to lose control for a moment. The public likes it when you politely and warmly remind reporters that you know what their game is and that they aren't going to win by getting you to break down under artificial pressure.

6. Agenda

This can really be called "Persistence with a specific goal." Instead of "let's see where this will take us," the agenda says "let's *get there* at any cost." The reporter is working to get you to make a specific statement. Your comments will help make the story "correct" from the reporter's standpoint, and give the story the right slant. In this case, the reporter's need and goal is to *get you to say it*. This relieves the reporter of having to say it—*you* already did.

Examples of "agenda"

A reporter told me that her first Washington, D.C., assignment for a major television network was to interview a high-level government official who had just announced that he was resigning his post in the Nixon administration. The assignment editor told her, "Get him to say he's leaving because of Watergate." She described the interview to me and it went something this way:

Q: Isn't it true that you're resigning because of Watergate?

A: I've been working 16-hour days. I haven't had any time for my wife and three young children. I decided that the time had come to be a real husband and father.

Q: Well, but Watergate helped you reach that conclusion didn't it?

A: I was motivated by a need to keep my marriage together and to get to know my kids.

Q: There's a lot of talk that it was really Watergate. Didn't it influence you in the slightest?

A: My wife needs me. My kids need me. They're the real reason I'm leaving.

The reporter felt defeated. She had failed. She went back with her videotape and cried. She couldn't force her editor's agenda on the subject. The interview didn't make it on the air. But consider this: Had the interviewee reacted in anger and said, *"I'm not resigning because of Watergate,"* the segment would have aired with the anchor saying, "Nixon aide denies resigning over Watergate," then during the interview we'd have heard:

Q: Isn't it true that you're resigning over Watergate?

A: I am not resigning over Watergate.

We'd have heard *resigning over Watergate* three times and that's the weed the audience would be left with. Score one more for the press.

7. The "What If"

The hypothetical question has "disaster" written all over it. It doesn't require an answer. It doesn't deserve an answer. But you have to make it clear to the audience that it is hypothetical, and be calm and warm in response. It even helps if you can demonstrate a sense of humor without appearing to be a "smart aleck." When CNN's Bernard Shaw pulled the trigger on presidential candidate Michael Dukakis, asking him if he'd still oppose the death penalty if Kitty Dukakis had been brutally raped and murdered, Dukakis would have scored points with a smiling, "Bernie, we wouldn't need a death penalty if I got my hands on him." Case closed. When Dan Quayle was asked what he would do as vice president if the president were assassinated, Quayle's, "I'd pray," seemed inept, given the facial reaction that made him appear to be groping. He might have turned it around with, "You ought to ask the president what he'd do if I were assassinated. After all, I'm the unpopular one." The question was so outlandish and so undeserving of an answer that a near-playful answer that didn't make light of the president's death would have put the public on notice that the reporter couldn't come up with a substantive question.

The "what if" question has lots of first cousins. Some of them are:

- "Who's to blame...?"
- "Whose fault is it...?"
- "Who's responsible...?"

Every news organization would gleefully print or air your comments that place blame. Even if you think you know the answer, be sure to make it clear that you're not a judge, not a jury, and certainly not God. You can even say that too many decent people have had careers and reputations destroyed by someone who decided to mouth off to a reporter.

Another cousin is "What really happened?" The suggestion here is that you know a lot more than you're willing to tell. Each technique is designed to hit a button.

If you allow yourself to get frustrated, angry, insulted, or stressed out, you're guaranteeing yourself an unflattering appearance on the evening news or one of the tabloids.

8. "That's a Wrap..."

These are famous last words. When you hear them your guard goes down. It's over. Well, it's not over 'til it's over. And that's when they're *gone.* Some reporters and their crews use it as a trick to be played on the unsuspecting. The words suggest that the camera and microphone are turned off and the interview is finished. Don't say another word except to exchange small-talk pleasantries, or what you see on the air may be what you said after you thought the game was over. Don't give them a victory in overtime. There's a simple, time-tested, foolproof rule: If you don't want to see it in print or hear it on the airwaves, *don't say it.*

9. The Clothesline

Many reporters will hang out a clothesline filled with questions. You're not expected to be able to remember each of four or five questions in one bundle of laundry. First answer the question that suits you best and then ask the reporter, "What else did you want to know?" I've even heard people say, "That's a lot of questions. Which one would you like me to answer?" And the audience subconsciously nods and says, "Right. That's really a mouthful of questions."

10. "It's Been Said..."

When the reporter knows that there may be a slander or libel lawsuit over what comes next, the opening words are "It's been said..." or "There are reports circulating that..." or "Rumor has it that...." An answer that begins with "Let me tell you what I know so far," or "Here are the facts as I understand them," or "Obviously someone is supplying you with misinformation," will help you over the bomb without detonating it. There are lots of other possibilities, as long as honesty remains the number-one priority.

11. Position

When you're outdoors in bright sunlight, the crew will rarely place the reporter looking directly into the sun. Don't let them do it to you. It will produce a pronounced squint, and an unwanted closed face. Insist on angling yourself into a position that will let you be natural. You and the reporter should be allowed to look at each other without either producing a grotesque look.

12. The Answer

I've been told about trainers who tell their clients, "This is your interview. Make sure you get your message out. Regardless of what you're asked, answer with one of these six prepared statements." My training urges you to answer the question that was asked, but do it from your perspective. Translate the question into what it would have been if the interviewer hadn't been trying to trip you up. That will let you do a commercial. My advice is that before you give your next interview, reread this chapter to give yourself an edge. It will help you give a winning interview.

Selling Yourself in the Classroom

Teachers, as do all those who speak to others as part of their jobs, often forget that the prime purpose of the teaching profession is communication. Teachers can lose sight of this within weeks of the first semester on the job because they must deal with a lot of externals that seem to have very little to do with communicating.

The Teacher as Administrator

If you're a teacher, no sooner do you report to work than you're faced with the realization that a teacher is not just a teacher. The job description says "teacher," but you're also a:

- Warden.
- Shrink.
- Surrogate parent.
- Traffic cop.
- Records-keeper (attendance-taker, grade-recorder, paper-grader, administrative flunky).
- Messenger.
- Cafeteria security guard.

And about a dozen other people.

The overwhelming responsibilities of the non-classroom, non-teaching aspects of the work may obscure your focus as a teacher.

What was a job you really looked forward to starts to resemble a nightmare of extraneous responsibilities.

I know.

I've been there.

Don't lose sight of the fact that teaching is your first priority, and teaching demands skillful communication techniques.

The Teacher as Communicator

Every dictionary synonym for *teach* suggests a receiver for the information being taught by the teacher: impart, instruct, inform, educate, inculcate, enlighten, indoctrinate, train.

The video operator for a California program I conducted put it this way: "The greatest teachers are the great storytellers." I couldn't agree more. Or to put it another way: students are members of an audience.

A teacher is in the classroom for one primary reason: to give information. *Give* is the key word here. It isn't enough to know your subject. It isn't enough to be a great source of information.

The secret to really good teaching is good communication, the ability to get the information from your mind into the student's mind. That takes dynamic delivery.

It requires the skills of the open face and the gesture.

It requires the ability to look and sound as if the most important thing in your life at this particular moment is the communication in your teaching.

I'm not saying you have to be a great entertainer. If you were, you'd be able to make huge bucks in show business. But selling yourself as a speaker is a performing art and is essential in front of a classroom.

Fresh Material

Ironically, one of the pitfalls of teaching is familiarity with your subject. After a while, teaching can become as routine as small talk. But what may be tiresome to you after you've been over the same material dozens of times is still brand new to the student. This is the point you must never forget.

In theater, actors are told about the "illusion of the first time" and taught the techniques they need to achieve this freshness. This is simply the ability to make the audience feel that you're telling this story, saying these words, communicating these ideas for the first time and spontaneously. It's a vital part of acting because every performance following opening night is a repeat, but it should still be as fresh and interesting as it was the first time.

Why has no one ever stressed that same notion with teaching? It deserves consideration. Every Algebra I class is essentially the same as every other Algebra I class. The teacher needs to keep the image of the "first time" in his or her presentation in order to make the material fresh and interesting for the students, who in fact are hearing it for the first time.

Most of us are what we are, and have certain academic strengths and weaknesses because a particular group of teachers excited us and another group turned us off.

A good teacher must have a tremendous desire and an excellent ability to get the message across to the student.

Dull teachers can make a bore out of exciting material, but interesting teachers, good teachers, can make magic out of what would otherwise seem to be very ordinary material.

Perhaps it would help if the designation "teacher" were given only to those who were interesting in the front of the classroom and a different name given to those who merely presented material by rote.

Enthusiasm and Knowledge

It might seem like a revolutionary idea, but think of what a difference it would make in our ability to educate if all teachers were required to develop good communication skills in addition to their academic requirements. It happened to me and I'm sure it's happened to you. There were times when going to school was a joy. And there were other times when you were literally sick before the school bell rang at the start of the day. The difference was almost always the teacher's ability to create interest and enthusiasm in the classroom, no matter what the subject.

If material seems to be boring to the teacher, it will be boring to the students, but the reverse isn't necessarily true. Just because the teacher is interested in the material doesn't necessarily mean the class will be interested.

The responsibility of the teacher is to get the class interested. This means making the classroom an exciting place to be. It also means that each day's lesson has to be presented in the most interesting, pleasant, vital, and exciting manner possible. When viewed in this light, teaching can be one of the most challenging and rewarding careers anyone could choose.

Teachers as Communicators

I did a training program for teachers in a major school system in the southwest. It took place the day before the fall term was to begin. There were 1,200 teachers attending the program. Two participants had prepared to present their opening-day classes in front of the group and knew they would be videotaped.

Each one greeted us as though we were the class and did the first five minutes of the lecture.

Before playing back the videotape to show them how they came across, I talked about the speaking techniques that make for great communication:

open face, open body, voice preparation, and confidence. Then we played back their demonstrations, watching them in the light of those techniques.

Both participants, along with the audience, saw strengths they should keep and weaknesses they should eliminate.

It Works!

When the two participants delivered the same opening a second time, the difference seemed to be magic. The second time around, they made a conscious effort to *open* their faces.

They gestured on their descriptive words.

They were alive.

They were dynamic.

They were dramatic.

They really cared about us.

Everyone was so delighted that they gave the two participants a standing ovation to express their pleasure with the improvement in their teaching skills.

And here's what everyone in the audience learned about good teachers:

- They should leave their personal problems and non-teaching responsibilities behind.

- They should remember that the student has never heard any of this before.

- They should make an event out of the class.

- If they enjoy themselves, their students will enjoy themselves—and learn.

- Above all, they could get more attention and have a greater impact if they stopped thinking about themselves as disciplinarians and remembered that their function is communication.

Again, if whoever is in the front of the room isn't communicating, that person is not a teacher. That's why I like to think of teaching not merely as a speaking process, but as a selling process too.

In no profession more than the teaching profession are these words more meaningful:

No one has the right to be dull.

S elling Your Product

Throughout this book, I've repeated several points that I consider vitally important. This chapter is the ultimate in redundancy because common sense says "no one will buy your product until and unless they like you." The more you understand that principle and work on your likability factor, the better your sales record will be.

Selling Your Product by Selling Yourself

Over the years, I've trained thousands of Merrill Lynch financial consultants. At first, the people I trained were professional people with several years of experience and above-average sales records. They reported that their sales shot through the roof after understanding the open face, eye contact, gesture, storytelling, personalizing, and appearing not as sales professionals, but as loving family members.

They convinced the people who run the training center that it would be the most useful to bring me to the new hires and give them all a better start. I can't tell you how satisfying it is to have so many people express gratitude for opening a door through common-sense principles.

The Need to Communicate

It helps to realize that we're all on trial constantly.

We're all running for public office every day.

We're all selling our ideas and ourselves all the time.

When there's a product involved, nothing is different, but there are a few special considerations.

Selling is the process of persuading a person or a group to buy a product or a service. The more beneficial to both, the more likely it is that the sale will be made and, more importantly, that each party will come away satisfied with the transaction. For a sale to happen and for customer satisfaction to be the final and enduring result, some basic principles apply.

Those Basic Principles

First, you've got to know your product. You've got to know it thoroughly and speak about it with confidence and authority. You also have to know the competition thoroughly. This allows you to speak well of your competition while emphasizing your own strengths.

Second, you have to believe in your company, your product, and yourself. You have to be proud to represent your company. It's obviously the best in its field. After all, it hired you.

Third, "ya gotta know the territory," as Meredith Willson said in one of the songs from *The Music Man.* That means you need to know who the decision-maker is and sell to that person. It's a total waste of time to make the sale and then discover that you have to make it again because you've been selling to the wrong person. I realize that sometimes you have to do it twice, but if once will do, why repeat?

The 3 I's

To accomplish these three steps, the good salesperson must have and exercise what salesman Steve Niven calls "The Three I's":

- Intelligence.
- Integrity.
- Initiative.

By intelligence, we're not talking about a high IQ. We're talking about sensitivity, timing, friendliness, warmth, and solid information, with a large dose of common sense thrown in.

Integrity is the hallmark of the salesperson who has long-term success. Yes, a lot of fly-by-night people make megabucks at other people's expense, but the customers of a salesperson with real integrity keep coming back because they know they'll get honesty, quality, price, and service. A person can't have just a little integrity. It's something you either have or you don't. And that's what the customer becomes aware of very early in the selling game. You have to have a good name, and the only way you get that and keep it is by having integrity.

Initiative is the ability to get in the door, to make the presentation in a unique, interesting, imaginative way, and to know you did a good job for yourself and the company, even if you didn't make the sale.

Selling as Communication

Why should selling a product be any different from selling yourself or your ideas? It isn't. A company is only as good as the people who represent it and, for the moment, you're the company. And, in almost every case, the client has to believe in you before believing in what you're selling. So, what should the client see?

- A warm person.
- A sincere person.
- An open person.
- An enthusiastic person.
- A trustworthy person.

The client also wants a positive person.

He wants you to tell him the good features of your product, not to bad-mouth the competition.

If there were problems in the past, don't blame the home office or the shipping department. Just take the initiative and be sure it doesn't happen again, or you can kiss that account goodbye.

Don't make claims or promises that can't be kept.

If you are the best and if you represent the best, your client will get what he buys.

He'll get it on time.

He'll be happy with it, *and* he'll welcome anything you bring him in the future.

You Can't Win 'Em All

Don't be discouraged by a series of "no sale" calls. You can't know why you didn't make the sale, and sometime it has nothing to do with you, your product, or your presentation. If you suspect it's you, then work at improving your selling techniques. But don't lose sight of other factors that may have caused the buyer to look elsewhere.

It's not outside the realm of belief in today's world that someone is "kicking back." The buyer may have a brother-in-law selling the same basic products. You may be dealing with a true status-quo person ("We've been buying Faunce Corporation widgets for 30 years and we're happy with them.").

There are reasons you'll never even dream of, so just press on, improve, grow, and do the best you can.

Don't Waste Their Time—or Yours

Time is an important commodity. Don't waste it. When you're making a sale, know all your facts.

- State them.
- Answer any questions.
- Ask for the order.
- Thank your client.
- Go.

Variety Is the Spice of Life

Vary your presentations. Keep them fresh. Use your imagination. Be creative. Dare to be different. This sets you apart from the pack and will help you make the sale.

Enjoy your work. Believe it or not, it's contagious. Just as when you make intellectual love to your audience and your audience loves you back, when you're having a good time working, it shows, and others enjoy your enjoyment.

Enjoy What You're Doing

I remember watching Ed McMahon, my favorite salesman, selling vegetable slicers the way he had done years before on the boardwalk in Atlantic City, New Jersey. It was such great fun for him that people who didn't need slicers—who didn't even want slicers—bought them to show that they enjoyed his enjoyment. It was their way of applauding him for a great show.

Now, you may not be selling slicers, but you are putting on a show for your client, so a key ingredient is the ability to have a good time doing it.

McMahon often said, "If I can point to it, I can sell it." He could just as easily have said, "If I can tell you about it, I can sell it to you." Not only was he a splendid performer, but he connected in that most important way: as the jovial, beloved family member.

The buyer doesn't want a professional salesperson. The buyer wants a son or daughter or grandchild.

If you've ever sold a house, the real estate agent you picked met all the likability criteria.

If you bought a car, remember what it was about the salesperson who convinced you to pick that brand, that dealership, and that model.

In all the seminars I've conducted, the technique I teach that has been most helpful to salespeople is the technique of the open face. Even the most successful salespeople in my teaching sessions agree that they found a new clue to helping themselves become believed, trusted, and, ultimately, even more successful. I urge you to work on this technique every chance you get. Your mirror may not buy what you have to sell, but your clients and customers will.

$\boxed{S}$ elling Yourself in the Job Interview

One of the most stressful speaking situations is the job interview. And, unless I miss my guess, we've all been through it one time or another. If you really need that job, if it seems your whole life depends on it, the stress can be almost unbearable.

I have a friend who worked hard all his life, earned a decent salary, and reached a prestigious position in his field. Suddenly, because of a merger, he found himself out of work; jobless. Because he and his wife had put several children through college and had supported more than one indigent family member, they had very few assets. Now, he had no job. After months of looking, his resume made an impression on a potential employer and he was asked to come in for an interview.

Desperation Can Kill the Deal

My advice to my friend (and you) was (and is), "Whatever you do, don't panic."

"But everything, everything, everything is riding on this one interview," you say.

Maybe so, but if you're desperate and it shows, you haven't got a chance. That piece of advice is really the key to success in the job interview and in every other form of communication. When an interviewer or an audience sees you squirm, becomes aware of your desperation, you're almost certain to be a loser.

I've painted a grim scenario, but my advice is equally true for the college student looking for the first post-graduation, full-time job.

It's true for the woman who's been out of the job market raising a family, who's decided that her sanity and/or her financial situation require her to get back into the money-earning world.

It's true for the man or woman who wants to change companies or jobs.

What is really important is the way you communicate, the way you're perceived by the person conducting the interview. Remember: Likability wins.

Wrong Impressions

The psychology involved in the typical job interview is false and destructive. It discourages honest communication. The interviewee tends to look on the interviewer as someone in a position of ultimate power, and this feeling grows in direct proportion to the real need for employment.

He controls my future.

My fate is in his hands.

He holds the key to restoring me to the ranks of respectability.

He is the supreme judge of my worth and value.

He has a secure job in a position of influence and power.

It's not fair.

Not only is all of this not true, but, also, the interviewee suspects that his own unemployed status or job search will be perceived by the interviewer as a flaw or weakness. After all, being unemployed or looking for another job (we think) is shameful, blameful, and a vulnerable condition.

It's a classic guilt trip.

These dynamics can be horrifying. "How on earth can I ever explain how smart and skilled and knowledgeable I am in a few minutes to a perfect stranger?"

To make it worse, quite often the interviewer's manner, style, and approach all reinforce these dynamics. The stress for the interviewee is intensified, approaching the unbearable.

In fact, the applicant who feels this desperation (and worse, shows it) will unwittingly magnify all these fears into a huge and haunting specter.

Desperation always manages to show itself in the eyes.

Insecurity is betrayed by the entire body.

The face and hands send all the signals you hope to avoid.

The voice quivers and trembles, and a mind in panic is in no condition to cope with the interview at hand.

What Can You Do?

First, as in any stressful situation, gain control of yourself by doing the breathing and relaxation exercises in Chapter 4.

Second, bring into play all of the basic communication skills you learned in earlier chapters. Use your face, your voice, and your body to gain control over the situation rather than let it gain control over you.

Next, consciously adopt a counter-psychology. What allows you to do this is the knowledge that the intimidating dynamics of the job interview are false.

They are negative.

They have no reality.

They are imagined and born of fear, stress, and intimidation.

Here are three factors to consider:

- Your worth and your value are in you. They have nothing to do with whether or not you are employed, holding a job, or earning money. You're the same person regardless of your situation.

- Your interviewer isn't intrinsically superior to you. Yes, because of the transient circumstances of the moment, he or she is more powerful than you are. But the interviewer's power isn't ultimate. There are other jobs, other employers out there.

You're a free person. You and your interviewer are essentially equal in two respects: You're both human beings and each may have something the other needs and wants. Only your roles are different. They could very well be reversed. The interviewer needs to fill the job vacancy as much as you need the job. Don't lose sight of the fact that you are also interviewing your interviewer about the job and about the company.

- You aren't just looking for a job. If you are, you could be making a world-class mistake. You're looking for the *right* job. You're looking for the job that will let you put your skills and experience to work most fully and productively, matching them to the needs of the employer. The purpose of the job interview, and never lose sight of this fact, is to determine whether those conditions prevail in this job.

Reaffirm Your Confidence

Once you have put the job interview in its proper perspective, you gain new confidence. You're not cocky, insolent, or impolitic; you are *confident.* You understand the dynamics of the interview. You've learned how to play a new game, and you can play to win.

Confidence is the key word. Externally, it will allow you to be friendly, open, interested, straightforward, and a good listener. Inside, you're alert, energized, and, on the deepest level, detached and objective. You're able to believe from the outset, "If this works out, that will be fine. If it doesn't work out, that will be okay, too. This one may not be the perfect one."

Confidence helps on every level. You come across as competent and poised. You're calm enough to think clearly and rationally. Your modest self-assurance is pleasant and attractive compared to the insecurity, nervousness, or over-eagerness of other candidates. You really shouldn't want the job unless it's right for you or if the employer doesn't have the right enthusiasm for adding you to the team.

An Expert's Advice

Jack Mannion, a friend who spent several years as a professional job counselor and whose help on the material for this chapter has been invaluable, offers the following tip:

If you're desperate for work, desperate for an income, any income, then take whatever job you can get that will bring in some money while the job search goes on. Work as a sales clerk in the evening. Take an early morning delivery job. Work on a clean-up crew at night. Whatever you do need never show up on your resume.

There is no such thing as a demeaning job; there are only people who consider themselves too good to do certain kinds of work. Overqualified, yes. Demeaning, no.

Once you have the right attitude about a job interview, there are certain strategies you can use both on your resume and during the interview itself that will go a long way toward guaranteeing your success.

Primary Interview Objectives

Identify Your Strongest Skills or Areas of Experience

Most of us are not totally one-dimensional. Unless we're just starting out in a career search or have had highly specialized technical careers, we probably have several strong suits. It's not unusual for someone to be skilled and have a background in more than one area such as:

- Planning.
- Organization.
- Production management.
- Personnel management.
- Budget and financial planning.
- System design.
- Sales.

- Marketing.
- Training and development.
- Editing.
- Public relations.
- Communications.

Analyze your work history to pinpoint precisely the central, basic categories of your skills and experience rather than the specific duties of a job you've held.

For example, you were an analyst/administrator of the XYZ Corporation rather than program officer in charge of impact statements for the office of Environmental Compliance.

The approach of highlighting your *general* skills has two main advantages:

First, it's flexible and you're flexible, depending on the needs of the potential employer.

Second, it stands alone, stripped of ties to your previous employer and open to future applications. As your interviewer, I'm not as interested in what your duties and responsibilities were in your last job as I am in what you can do for me now.

Cite Specific Examples of Your Accomplishments in Measurable Terms

Give numbers that quantify what you were responsible for, how effective you were, the changes you brought about, the volume you handled, the number of people you supervised, the increase in sales or productivity, the size of your budget, and the scope of your function. Use whatever yardstick is appropriate, such as degrees of growth, improvement, or accuracy; honors and citations; promotions and bonuses; decrease of complaints; increase in income, membership, output, or stock value. These kinds of objective measurements say more about your ability and actual accomplishments than any claims you may make. And wherever possible, use the techniques of storytelling, anecdotes, and personal examples.

Learn What You Can About Your Potential Employer and the Business

Check out the company's Website. Learn what you can about the company, its problems, strengths, plans, operations, goals, and past successes and past failures. There may even be information available on the company's hiring practices. This will allow you to orient your statements to the company's needs and also establish that you've done some homework and know what you're talking about.

Getting across these three points is the primary objective in any interview. No matter what the interviewer wants to talk about, you want that person to hear what you can do, how well you can do it (or how well you've done it in the past), and how your skills and experience relate to and can benefit that company.

Don't let any questions, comments, ramblings, or war stories distract you from making your points. Even if the interviewer asks the wrong questions, you can give the right answers.

I have to stress this point because most interviewers are not good at interviewing. You won't always be given the opportunity to tell your story as you'd planned, so you may have to create that opportunity. This isn't usually maliciousness on the interviewer's part, but rather ineptness.

My advice is to never leave an interview without having made your best case—unless, of course, you've lost all interest in the job that's available.

Using all the tact, warmth, and subtlety you can muster, you have to take control of the interview, always allowing the interviewer to continue to feel in control. You must keep returning to what you can do, how well you can do it, and how that might apply to the interviewer's needs. Don't linger over a general conversation. Keep the spotlight focused on the subject of the interview: you.

But don't forget to be a good, attentive listener.

The Way the Game Is Played

There are two kinds of interviews: the general interview and the specific job interview.

The general interview is aimed at establishing and developing leads. You want someone of some consequence to know that you're available and have something to offer. It may turn out that this contact does become interested in hiring you, which would be an ultimate scenario. Otherwise, your attitude is "I'm not expecting you to offer me a job. Rather, I'd like to explore with you where someone with my background and skills might be useful to someone in your field or someone you know who might be interested."

This immediately lowers the interviewer's resistance. He's off the hook and is only being asked for advice and possible leads. He doesn't have to face the problem of turning down another nice person and is flattered into being in a position we all love, that of the expert. It also opens the door to his hearing a straightforward presentation of your skills and experience. How can he make a suggestion to you or advise someone with your background without learning what that background is?

There are two possible outcomes to this sort of interview: It becomes an actual job interview (with the discovery of what a wonderful addition you would be to his team) or you turn it into leads to other interviews. There is, of course, a third possibility—a dead-end failure—but that's likely to be your own fault.

Ask for Help and Guidance

Even here, guilt and wasted time may be avoided simply by pressing for other leads. "Who else do you think I might talk to in order to explore other possibilities in my field?" Get names, titles, and other information to the extent that you can without being pushy. Ideally, you may even impress your interviewer enough that he'll volunteer to telephone his leads on your behalf and let them know they'll be hearing from you.

Door-opening of this sort is devoutly to be hoped for, if not actively pursued. Your contact can hardly call his friend or associate on your behalf without saying something favorable about you. Your ultimate objective here is to create a network of contacts who are familiar with your abilities, who are impressed by your credentials and by you, and who know you're available. Remember: More good jobs come through such networks than through the want ads. A friend, or a friend of a friend, can be an invaluable lead to the right job.

If your general interview becomes a job interview, it means you've done well and can shift gears. The job interview usually has a predictable structure:

- You describe your background and skills.

- The interviewer describes the job.

- You relate your skill and experience to the job.

- If the interviewer becomes interested in you, then it is your turn to interview him or her in detail about the job. Find out what you can about the responsibilities, authority, opportunity, job description and flexibility, budget, supervisor, staff and associates, company standards and expectations, resources, procedures, personalities, prospects for the future, and anything else that might be relevant to you.

- You and the interviewer discuss salary, benefits, amenities, and other details.

- Intermission. Rarely is a job offered, or accepted, on the spot. Both parties need additional time to think about it. The interviewer will check your references. You'll look over the company materials and publications. Often other interviews will occur during this break.

- Offer and acceptance. More discussion and exchange of information. Anything to be further negotiated regarding salary, perks, vacation, and the like are hashed out here. Then both parties make the decision.

Performing Effectively

Although the circumstances may be slightly different, the job interview, as are many speaking situations, is essentially a matter of communication—the way you present yourself and your ideas and the way they are perceived by your audience, in this case, the interviewer. So, naturally, the same techniques and strategies apply in both situations.

If you've mastered the use of your face, your gestures, and your voice, if you're prepared and confident, and if you send the winning signals in the way you look and the way you dress, you can master any job interview that comes your way.

A Final Piece of Advice

A job interview can be, and often is, a kind of mini-confrontation. An interviewer, just as an aggressive reporter might, may ask you questions that are difficult, if not impossible, to answer. But you can turn negative questions into positive answers.

Pause, look at the interviewer, and then give honest, positive answers that will present you in the best possible light.

If your interviewer zings you with, "What do you consider your greatest weakness?" give it a positive twist with something such as, "Most of the people I work with think I'm too dedicated to my job" or "My attention to detail seems to bother some colleagues, but usually not the boss."

If you're asked, "What's the minimum salary you'll accept?" don't be afraid to toss it back. "I think I should be offered whatever salary the job is worth to the company. What figure did you have in mind?"

"What's the biggest mistake you've made professionally?" Turn it around: "I once trusted a person more than I should have. His actions hurt both me and my business associates. It taught me to check people out."

"Don't you honestly believe you're overqualified for this position?" If you believe the interviewer's perception is wrong, you might try, "Not unless you've got a lid on the job, the salary, and the responsibility that I'm not aware of."

A job interview is a one-on-one situation and, just as the interviewer is sizing you up by the signals you send, you can size up the company by carefully observing his signals. Is he open, considerate, and courteous? Or is he closed, uninterested, harsh, or even hostile? It won't take you long to figure that one out. And if the latter is true, you'd probably rather not work for the company he represents. In fact, he may soon be out of a job.

It Works!

For several years, I've done many programs for the training arm of Arthur Young, now Ernst & Young. As I was working on the first edition of this book, I got a letter from Alice Rice, one of the breakout leader trainers who had worked with me on dozens of occasions. Here's what she wrote:

> Dear Arch,
>
> I began working with Colleen (a job search consultant) in February of 2001 when I determined it was time for a career change. After about three weeks of working to prepare a resume, build my campaign, and identify prospective employers, Colleen decided it was time for a mock interview. I had been trained by the best for the best in presentation techniques. To my surprise, I was nervous and anxious about the 20-minute video we were going to tape to allow a critique of my interviewing for a new job.
>
> As Colleen was asking me questions related to "your best experience," "what you are most proud of," "what can you offer my company," etc., I kept some very simple thoughts in mind. All of these came to me through my training with you. From the time we met in May of 1988, you truly changed the way I present myself to others. Your best

advice was given succinctly and with humor. I learned to be natural, flexible, and have a good time! I learned to speak in common language and to eliminate jargon. That is just what I did in the mock interview. I listened carefully to the questions and provided natural and fun examples that anyone could understand. I explained my past 18 years with enthusiasm and easy-to-follow descriptions. I had a good time and it showed.

At the end of 15 minutes, Colleen stopped the taping. She looked up, somewhat startled but pleased, and asked if she could keep the tape for demonstrations to future clients. She indicated that it was the best mock interview she had seen in seven years. I welcomed her enthusiasm and honesty. I knew I had done well! I ultimately received a job offer after just one interview.

The skills you taught me over the years yielded a confidence that I could not have mustered otherwise. Your techniques really work.

Once Again—It Works!

I was checking into a Portland, Oregon, hotel to do a presentation the following day. The desk clerk said, "Mr. Lustberg, you have a message," and handed me an envelope. I figured it was from my client concerning the program, but instead, it was a letter. It said:

I heard you were coming to Portland. I wanted to see you to tell you this personally, but I have to be away. With your training, I feel I really learned to present myself and the proof is that I applied for a new job—got it—and doubled my salary. Before that, every job I tried for went to someone else. Thanks for your help.

Selling Yourself When Testifying

There was a time when our knowledge of legal procedures and the courtroom was limited to TV programs (*Law and Order*) or films (*Philadelphia*). Now, with so many people suing or investigating each other, and with most of us embracing and speaking out for causes, we may find ourselves involved in a court case or a legislative proceeding.

To testify effectively requires considerable skill.

As does a television or a radio interview, delivering testimony takes place on "foreign soil." We're asked to appear in strange surroundings that can adversely affect our ability to play the game. Also, as with the radio or TV interview, giving testimony is often a confrontational situation. You may have a patient and friendly questioner who guides you through your testimony, or you may have an impatient and hostile questioner who is trying to prove you are lying through your teeth.

What are you supposed to say?

How are you supposed to react?

In court and in hearings, every appearance is different, but the communication skills are similar.

The Deposition

Before a trial begins, more often than not, depositions are taken. A deposition is simply a pretrial statement made under oath before attorneys for both sides and a clerk. There is no jury and usually no judge. Supposedly, the deposition helps prepare the two sides for the courtroom and shortens the trial time. The key words here are **under oath.** If you fail to tell the truth in a deposition, it's as bad as if you lied in the actual courtroom. Perjury is perjury regardless of where it happens.

The entire difference between the deposition and courtroom testimony is that in the deposition, only substance counts. There is no judgmental audience except for the attorneys, and they can't acquit or convict. They can't bring the case to its conclusion. So, only the mind is involved.

Face, body, and voice hardly come into play in the deposition. It is a confrontational situation, however, so the pause is once again your most effective weapon. When you are asked a question, think *before* you speak. Pause, take aim, get ready, fire. And, needless to say, your answer should be the truth.

It probably seems that I'm oversimplifying, but honesty and the pause are the only tools you'll need in the deposition.

The pause gives you the opportunity to consider the question, its meaning, and its consequences before you answer.

Being honest means you won't perjure yourself. If you tell the truth, you never have to remember what you said.

If you don't know, say so.

If you don't understand the question, say so.

And the pause in every scenario allows your attorney to interject with a point or an objection.

The Courtroom Trial

With the presence of a judge and possibly a jury to determine the outcome of a case, the skills of face, body, and voice become vitally important in giving testimony. Yes, the ground rules for the deposition also apply here, but how the jury perceives you is critical.

Don't forget that the jury is an audience and it can like you, dislike you, feel sorry for you, or be neutral to you. Your job, along with being truthful, is to be *liked,* because the jury will then believe you're telling the truth.

No one will ever know how many people guilty of heinous crimes have been set free because the jury liked them. Conversely, I'll bet a lot of innocent people have been convicted because the jury thought they looked as though they were criminals. But most juries, as are most audiences, are not easily deceived. They believe what they hear if what they see makes it believable.

The open face, the genuine and appropriate gesture, and the warm, friendly voice are the weapons most likely to help you win a jury to your side. If you need a villain, let it be the opposing attorney.

Now that cameras have invaded courtrooms in most high-profile trials, we're getting plenty of chances to see winners and losers up close and personal.

When you're on the stand, take a short pause before answering even the simplest question, and answer in a full sentence.

- "What is your name?"
  (Pause) "My name is...."

- "What is your address?"
  (Pause) "I live at...."

- "How long have you lived there?"
  (Pause) "I've been there since...."

Now the adversarial attorney has been put on notice. This witness will not be intimidated. This witness will not be tricked into blurting out answers. This witness knows what he's doing.

Self-Control

Appearing as a witness in a trial is obviously a stressful situation. So, before you testify, use proper breathing techniques for relaxation and control. If you look nervous and apprehensive, it might easily be mistaken for dishonesty. Think about people you've seen moistening their lips and shifting their eyes back and forth. They look intimidated and often seem to be groping for a way out or a dishonest answer.

Stick to the Essentials

Three rules to follow during your testimony—answering *only* the question that has been asked:

- Don't elaborate.
- Don't volunteer information.
- Always be brief and to the point.

It is, after all, the opposing attorney's job to discredit your testimony. It is your job to convince the jury that you're telling the truth.

As in any confrontation, you can turn negative questions into positive answers. And the communication skills of mind, body, and voice will do the rest in convincing the jury to decide in your favor.

It's not unusual for clients to tell me they did better than they thought they would. Several have even been congratulated by the attorney for the other side, telling them how good they were.

My son-in-law is an osteopath who frequently is asked to appear as an expert witness in workmen's compensation cases. He says that now that he's worked on the communication techniques I teach, the opposition lawyers are asking him after a trial ends if they can call on him as a witness in the future.

Congressional Testimony

An appearance before a committee of the U.S. Senate or House of Representatives is unlike any other experience. We've seen many examples of this on television. Some have been good; most have been terrible. The most familiar image is that of the witness who opens his attaché case, takes out an 80-page manuscript, hunches over the text, and says to the page,

"Mr. Chairman, members of this distinguished committee, my name is..." and on he drones until the last word is read in a dull monotone and everybody has fallen asleep.

How to Stand Out

There's no excuse for that kind of testimony. Very few people, including professional lobbyists, realize there's a regulation on the books that says that testimony before Congress will be a summary of what's been previously submitted. The person who reads the entire submission in a dull monotone is being just plain rude to Congress and is in violation of the rules.

If you're called upon to testify before Congress, first submit the full text of your statement, as required, 48 or 72 hours before your appearance. Second, prepare a *very brief* summary of that statement for oral delivery. Put it in short, snappy sentences, to be spoken rather than read. Then begin your testimony, after the protocol, with, "You have my full statement in front of you. Let me briefly summarize the highlights of that paper." Your listeners might even be induced to pay attention after that, knowing you plan to be mercifully brief and courteous.

Here is a brief rundown of some of the things I think your testimony should be:

- Honest.
- Positive.
- Brief.
- Simple.
- Logical.
- Well-organized.
- Well-delivered.
- Anecdotal rather than statistical.
- A concise statement of your position.

And, of course, in your delivery, all of the communication skills are a necessity: the open face, appropriate gestures, voice control, directness, and courtesy. When you consider how much of Congress's time is spent in hearings, you'll realize how practical these guidelines are and how much better your chances of really getting your message across will become.

The Local Hearing

A hearing on a local issue is the scenario most of us are likely to encounter. It's the least intimidating arena and certainly the most familiar. It's also the one that we are more willing to become involved with. After all, a local issue is one that affects us directly and personally.

But, here again, I know people who are so intimidated by the public-speaking situation that they've refused to be active participants in local issues. They won't speak out at public meetings because they have that terrible debilitating fear: the fear of making a fool of themselves in public. It's an unreasonable fear, but that knowledge doesn't change anything.

Using good communication skills will make public speaking easier.

The Right Beginning

Once more, I urge you to start off with proper breathing. It's the first step in the process of throwing off stress and gaining control of yourself.

Be prepared. That alone will increase your self-confidence enormously. Concentrate on making the briefest possible statement of your position. Five words usually have far more impact than 5,000.

Be open.

Be honest, direct, and courteous.

Be personal. Tell the assembled group what this action will mean to them, their community, their pocketbooks, their neighborhoods. This kind of information has impact.

A local hearing is usually much less formal than a legislative hearing. Use the lack of formality to your advantage. Observe any protocol, but be as informal as you feel will help your cause. And talk quietly. Even if the issue is highly charged and the hearing is adversarial, don't get angry. Don't lose your temper.

Above all, remember the rules of the confrontation.

Turn negative questions into positive answers.

If you pause and think before you speak, your words will have even greater impact.

Get Involved

If you've been consumed by fear and have refused to participate in local issues, remember that your viewpoint is just as important as anyone else's. By practicing the skills and techniques of good communication that apply in any speaking situation, you will be able to make a difference in your community by getting your message across.

It Works!

A developer I worked with recommended me to a friend in another city who was proposing a huge new development to a rather hostile city council. I got the call and we worked on his prepared statement and the questions he was likely to be handling. He was thrilled with the positive result. He subsequently had me work with him and his staff on his run for governor and then again on his reelection campaign. He learned to come across as likable and competent, and it resulted in good luck.

Selling Yourself in Meetings

Meetings are the staple of the American business diet. If you could grow good ones, you'd make a fortune. And if you could make every meeting productive, you'd be acclaimed a wizard—nothing less than a Merlin.

Every meeting has its natural barriers to success, including the following:

- Poor facilities.
- Technical equipment breakdowns.
- Uncomfortable surroundings.
- Boring people.
- Bad planning.
- Dull speakers.
- Unsavory refreshments.
- Unskilled chairpersons.
- A lack of direction.
- Digressions from the agenda.
- Professional troublemakers in attendance.
- Unfunny jesters.
- Unessential interruptions to prove someone's importance.

The list is endless, but the fact remains that meetings are the most frequent way in which we communicate with our colleagues and coworkers, our superiors and subordinates. If meetings fail, there has been a failure of communication.

Make Your Meeting a Success

Why should a meeting be different from any other speaking situation? It isn't. Someone talks and others listen. There are hundreds of reasons for a meeting's failure. But there's only one reason why a meeting is successful: Something specific was accomplished, and everyone in the room knew it and went away better off because of it. Usually, the person in the front of the room, the person in charge of the meeting, the chief speaker, is primarily responsible for the outcome.

What It Takes

Words alone do not a successful meeting make. Skillful, dynamic presentations do, whether you are the chairman, the chief speaker, or a participant. The way you present yourself and your ideas, the way you communicate, can make all the difference between just getting through a meeting and getting the results you had hoped for.

You know the difference I'm talking about. We've all been sorry we had to attend many of the meetings we've gone to, and we've been to a few that really excited us.

The meetings we left feeling that something had really been accomplished usually had an exciting, outstanding, dynamic chairperson.

Compelling.

Spellbinding.

A person who reached us on a personal, intellectual, and emotional level.

Was that person a natural?

Was there some special genius?

Maybe, but probably not.

Most of the really skilled communicators got where they are by working at developing their speaking skills.

As with all speaking skills, meeting skills can be acquired. More than that, they must be acquired. Today's work environment assigns more and more of us the task of opening our mouths in front of colleagues.

We give reports, briefings, instructions, and introductions.

We serve on or we chair committees and task forces.

We participate in meetings, seminars, and workshops.

In every one of these scenarios, we're expected to be active participants—to speak up.

Why Me?

Of all the speaking situations, the ones with the most riding on them are the professional ones. So colleagues, peers, bosses, and fellow professionals become the enemy. We're so petrified by the fear of failure that we close up, tighten up, and do all the wrong things. We tend to let stress overcome us rather than overcoming stress.

Don't Let Self-Doubts Destroy Your Effectiveness

Instead of attacking the problems, we often succumb to them. We think we're out of our league when we are expected to conduct a dynamic meeting. Our hyperactive imaginations scream our inadequacies. "I'm not good enough." "I'll really louse up and they'll laugh at me." "The boss won't think I'm authoritative enough." We produce an endless list of reasons why we may fail, including, "I'll be so nervous I'll forget to zip my fly."

Notice that the focus is turned inward, on ourselves. We see ourselves through the magnifying glass of fear and confusion. Every misplaced hair makes us think, "I look like a punk rocker." Our deep-seated anxieties set off all kinds of alarms. Our confidence, if we ever had any, disappears. We envision being publicly exposed as dumb, phony, wrong, inadequate, incompetent, and worse. We're stark naked in a meeting room filled with fully clothed people.

Although this scenario may seem exaggerated for some people, it's no less true for others. We look upon ourselves and see the worst.

We forget that, when we're the audience, we don't look at other front-of-the-room speakers in the same searching, scorching light. There's the key to overcoming our fear—that and breathing to relax and regain control of ourselves.

Expect to Succeed

The truth is that the audience doesn't care about the things you may consider physical imperfections. They will accept you as you are.

Yes, you should look your best.

Of course, you should dress neatly and inconspicuously, but your colleagues aren't looking at your weight or your hair or your nose or your teeth. If they know you, they're used to seeing you as you really are, warts and all. If they don't know you, they may take a quick inventory of your appearance and leave it at that, unless you begin to bore them.

In other words, self-consciousness is a self-centered waste of good energy. What the attendees do care about is your performance. That's where your concern and energy ought to be directed.

As in any speaking situation, your audience will give you, from the very outset, the benefit of the doubt.

The chairman is expected to be the chairman.

The invited speaker must have something to share.

The report-giver is presumed to know the project being reported on.

More than that, the group *wants* the chairman to be effective, the speaker to be interesting and informative, the instructor to be knowledgeable.

Your Cheering Section

In short, audiences invest the person with the qualities that go with his role. This phenomenon is a tremendous asset to you. The group quite matter-of-factly assumes that you know what you're about. For their attitude to change, you've got to *prove them wrong.* Conversely, if you perform more or less as they expect, you confirm their expectations and strengthen their acceptance of you.

What this means is that you can step out of yourself and into a speaker's role with the support and encouragement of the group. Act otherwise and you lose support automatically.

Be aware that these attitudes are created not by who you are, but rather by self-interest.

People don't want to waste their time or be bored.

The attendees want the meeting to go well for their own sakes. This automatically spells support for you and you can count on it.

It's Up to You

On the other hand, if you're preoccupied with yourself rather than the group and the event, you'll soon feel the positive vibrations converting to the sort of negative energy that causes cold sweat and a longing for oblivion.

So forget yourself.

Concentrate on your role.

Remember: All communication is sharing ideas, an intellectual act of love. You can't give yourself totally to your audience when your concentration is on yourself.

Many of us are reluctant to play a role. We don't want to be considered actors. If we do, our audience will think we're phonies. At the same time, we fear that our real selves will automatically be rejected. Both visions are false.

The underlying reason for every successful public performance is the communicator's ability, at least partially, to forget about himself and his imagined shortcomings and concentrate on the event, his role in it, and the audience to which he's delivering. It's the trademark of all successful communication. Remember that, and you'll succeed. Worry about a hair being out of place, and you'll validate your fear of failure.

What Does the Group Expect?

Leadership is the first quality. From chairpersons, discussion leaders, speakers, and instructors, the group wants leadership. During your time as chairperson or speaker, you're presiding. You're the one in charge. You have the right to control what happens and the obligation to see that it's effective. Sins against good leadership include:

- Lack of control.

- Lack of preparation.

- Rambling or boring presentations.

- Indecisiveness.

- Vagueness.

- Disorganization.

- Unclear objectives.

- Lack of sensitivity to the needs and wants of the group.

- Running over time.

Implicit in the list is the harsh fact that the person up front must know what he or she is doing and do it well. So make your presentation with warmth, authority, and assurance.

Do it efficiently and effectively.

Do it on behalf of the audience and be responsive to its needs and interests.

This isn't said to intimidate or frighten the newcomer, but to emphasize the need for competence in the speaking skills talked about throughout this book.

Cockiness is no less doomed to failure than a publicly displayed inferiority complex. You have a responsibility to your audience to know how to do your job well and to be responsive to the people present.

If I had to select the two items that destroy most meetings, I'd choose dull presiders and lack of sensitivity to the needs and wants of the group.

Content—real meat, not watery gruel—is the substance of your presentation. The virtues of a good presentation include:

- Solid information.

- Reliable data.

- Logical organization.

- Plain language.

- Sharply etched conclusions and recommendations.

- Examples relevant to the group's experience.

- Clear direction and purpose.

- An opportunity for the group to question and discuss what's been said.

- A chance for the group to get something of value for itself.

Skill and style—the way you present yourself and your ideas—is no less important than what you have to say. The way you speak, move, act and react, and the way you relate to the group can all either spell success or failure for the meeting.

In a more formal situation, there's usually a certain distance between you and your audience.

In a meeting, that distance is considerably diminished and, from the moment you walk into the room until the moment you walk out, you're *on*.

The Meeting as Communication

Basically, there are five types of meetings, most of which have overlapping functions and purposes:

▣ **Information meetings.** These are intended to deliver or exchange information. The boss has announcements to make. A federal agency wants to tell interested parties about upcoming regulations. The CEO expects the department heads to brief each other on the recent progress and plans for the next calendar period. A manager wants to exchange thoughts with other managers.

▣ **Decision-making meetings.** These are meetings in which a group negotiates or builds a consensus in order to arrive at a decision.

▣ **Instruction meetings.** These include training and educational programs of all kinds, meetings to issue directives and assignments, and events intended to result in change or action on the part of the participants.

▣ **Motivation meetings.** People's hearts and minds have to be won. They must be moved to respond. Buy this soap. Stop smoking. Improve your sales by learning these new techniques. Use these manuals and do better. Give us your support. Join our team. Whatever the subject area, these are meetings to persuade, cajole, motivate, inspire, and induce a desired action.

▣ **Social meetings.** If a meeting is purely social, it's often held to reward certain team members for exceptional performance. But more often than not, the annual meeting or team meeting is held with the social aspect as just one of its purposes. The Internal Revenue Service has seen to that by requiring an organization to have some official business purpose for any portion of the meeting that it claims as tax-deductible.

You Make the Difference

Almost every meeting you attend combines one or several of the five purposes. But whatever its purpose, the success or failure of the meeting depends upon the success or failure of the communication between the members of the group. Conceive of meetings as communication and you'll begin to think of them in a new and productive light. Whatever other role you are asked to play, you have to function as a communicator. No other concept of yourself—executive, taxpayer, expert, supervisor, professional—is half as pertinent and essential as the fact that you are a *communicator*.

Statistics show that most professionals spend more than 50 percent of their work time in meetings. Some sources cite a figure closer to 65 percent. And among professionals, it is almost unanimous that most meetings they attend have been a waste of time. Why? Because their leaders or speakers failed to communicate. What a colossal waste of everybody's time!

People who go to meetings offer us their time and attention.

They often pay for the privilege of attending.

They almost always leave important work behind.

They deserve genuine efforts at professionalism in platform behavior.

No one has the right to be dull for any reason—not because of greater importance or a busy schedule, not because of expertise superior to the audience's, and not even because of shyness or lack of skill.

As Jack Mannion, former executive director of the American Water Works Association, said, "If speakers are not willing to make the effort necessary to achieve at least a modicum of good technique and authentic communication, they have no right on the platform."

If You're the Leader, Lead

Whether you are the leader or a speaker, giving the attendees what they deserve requires the techniques as described earlier in this book: style, skill, preparation, and confidence.

As a leader, you have additional responsibilities.

A meeting can't just happen by itself simply because a group of people has assembled at your invitation or command.

You have to plan everything from "good morning," down to "this meeting is adjourned."

You have to make sure the technical details work.

You have to have and stick to an agenda.

To put it into English, you have to know what you want to get done and then do it.

You have to start on time and keep the meeting moving so that you can end it on schedule.

You've got to know the ideas you want to communicate and the best way to deliver them.

In addition to all that, a number of other factors, and how well you've thought them through, will determine the success or failure of the meeting.

The Site

Comfort and convenience should determine your choice of site. And remember: As soon as you move out of your office, your boardroom, or another facility in your headquarters, you're on foreign soil. That's true even if you're in a hotel where you've had lots of previous meetings, a friend's office where you've been dozens of times, or a local school auditorium or classroom where you've held meetings before. Something about the off-premises site or the personnel working there is different.

Leave Nothing to Chance

You need to plan for the inevitable surprises. If you need a lectern, a microphone, a flip chart, a projector—*anything*—make sure it's there, it works, and that you and your technician have rehearsed with it. That may seem so basic that it hardly deserves mention, but we've all been to meetings where "no problem" became famous last words.

When I conduct one of my training sessions, I'm in the room where my program is scheduled, with my video operator, at least an hour before starting time.

As soon as I'm booked, the client gets my equipment requirements along with the contract for my services. The meeting planner and my assistant talk whenever there are questions. When necessary, we're in touch with the site staff in advance.

Microphones, recorders, video playbacks? The more complicated the equipment you plan to use, the more there is that can go wrong.

The message is simply this: *No amount of checking is too much.*

Take absolutely nothing for granted. But don't panic when something does go wrong.

If the attendees aren't aware of a problem, there isn't any.

There may be some grief and anxiety for you and the technical staff, but, as long as the audience isn't aware of it, the program has a better chance for success.

The Occasion

The occasion obviously influences your choice of site and the way you conduct a meeting. For a small, informal meeting or lunch, choose the appropriate setting and encourage everyone to participate. The success of a large meeting mainly depends on the total control of the chairperson, without the audience being aware of its lack of participation. Whatever the occasion, your audience will have expectations that you must meet.

The Purpose

The reason for your meeting determines how and where it takes place. Make sure all three factors work together. An auditorium may be appropriate for information and instruction meetings but not for decision-making and social meetings. You can't expect to build a meaningful consensus toward making an important decision at a cocktail party, nor can you expect colleagues and coworkers to get to know each other better if you don't give them the time and the freedom to do so.

The Number and Types of Attendees

The more of them, the harder your job and, obviously, the more attention you need to pay to details. A few notes might help. Discourage the use of slides, charts, graphs, overhead projections, and other visual aids, especially in large meeting rooms. The people who sit in the back have a hard enough time seeing the speaker, let alone a lot of mechanical devices. And when you light a room for slides, the speaker is very often left in the dark. I believe a speaker is his own best visual aid. A really dynamite presenter doesn't need so-called help.

My rule is this: *Unless the visual tells your story better than you can, scrap it. A picture may be worth a thousand words, but when it doesn't do a thing for the audience's understanding, a visual aid becomes a cop-out and a distraction.*

Make Introductions Count

Watch out, too, for the "introduction trap." We feel that every speaker needs to have his whole life story told to the audience.

Wrong!

The shorter the better, providing two qualifications are met:

1. The audience should be eager to hear this person based on your introduction.

2. The speaker should be made proud to have been invited.

I've had the misfortune of having the presiding officer read my bio in detail. Yet, after the program, people still asked, "What did you do before you became a speech consultant?" It was all said, but nobody heard. Then there was the time when an introducer said, "Last March I saw our speaker do a training session and I said, 'We've got to bring him to our meeting.' I got the best information I've ever received at a convention program, and I'm certain you'll say the same. So please welcome our speaker, Arch Lustberg." He made the audience want to hear me. He made me feel proud to be there. It took about 10 seconds. It couldn't have been better.

Continuity

Even the most carefully planned meeting can still wander off course without the proper leadership *during* the meeting. Here are some tips to keep your meetings on course:

- Start on time. Don't punish promptness.

- Have a wonderful welcome ready. If you haven't been able to greet everyone personally at the door because of the sheer numbers, be sure to prepare a warm, friendly, sincere welcome.

- State the objective of the meeting. Even if the group has a detailed published agenda, briefly cover the highlights.

- Get everyone involved. Encourage participation. Even in large meetings this can be done by asking the attendees to fill out questionnaires.

- Ask leading questions. Call on silent types, but don't embarrass them. Sidestep the domineering talkers.

- Tie agenda items together. Provide links from one point to another. Offer periodic summaries.

- Venture tentative conclusions or agreements. Submit them as your understanding of what's been said so far for the group's approval.

- Watch for nonverbal signals. If you sense disapproval, strong agreement, boredom, skepticism, or objections, call for comment.

- Be nonjudgmental. You are the moderator, the traffic cop. Lead the group toward your desired objective, but don't try to dictate the outcome.

- Keep on time. Keep the subject matter on track. Without appearing rude, cut through digressions and irrelevancies.

- Communicate your genuine respect for every member of the group and what they have to say. Having established this connection, they'll tolerate and support your efforts to control digressions and other roadblocks and work with rather than against you to achieve the desired objective.

- End on time. Even better, end early.

Some Additional Tips

- Force yourself to listen.

- Concentrate.

- Pay attention.

- Don't anticipate what's coming next.

- Above all, don't finish other people's sentences—no matter how slowly or deliberately they speak.

- Ask questions.

- Be sure you understand what's just been said, and make sure the group understands what you're saying.

If you're open and honest and put into practice all the other rules and techniques of good communication, you'll encourage everyone else in the group to do the same. As the leader of a meeting, or as a participant when it's your turn to speak, remember that you're the spark plug that keeps the engine running and the meeting on course toward its desired destination.

A friend gave me a wonderful thought to share with you: *"Maybe there's no spark in the organization if there's no spark in the meeting."*

12-Step Guide to Make Your Next Meeting a Success

1. If there's no important information to exchange, don't hold a meeting.

2. Help attendees be prepared.

3. Check the meeting site early.

4. Start your meetings on time.

5. Set the right tone.

6. Use an agenda.

7. Encourage participation.

8. Remember: Our minds live in bodies.

9. Watch for non-verbal signs.

10. Beware of the signals you send.

11.   Hone your presentation.

12.   End on time.

Step 1: If There's No Important Information to Exchange, Don't Hold a Meeting

If this is the only rule we follow, we'll be ahead of the game. But we can (and should) do a lot more to turn meetings from wastes of time into productive time.

Step 2: Help Attendees Be Prepared

You'll improve the quality of your meeting, and reduce the odds of needing a follow-up session, by encouraging everyone to come prepared. They should know the subject of the meeting and exactly what's expected of them.

Will this be a one-sided transfer of information or an exchange of information? Will attendees be expected to just listen and absorb, or will they be asked to contribute knowledge and ideas? They should know up front. The best communicators are even better when they've had a chance to prepare a clear, concise presentation.

Step 3: Check the Meeting Site Early

You or another problem-solver should arrive early to check the physical set-up. You'll want a checklist of items that must be present and in working order and the names and phone numbers of those responsible for getting them there.

Step 4: Start Your Meetings on Time

Don't punish punctuality. Those who've dropped or postponed other business for your meeting shouldn't have to cool their heels waiting for stragglers. If they do, they'll soon get the message. They'll begin arriving later, and later, and later.... If you dare to start your meetings on time, even when some attendees haven't arrived, late-comers will become the rare exception, not the rule.

Step 5: Set the Right Tone

Arrive early for your own meeting to greet attendees individually as they arrive, unless your group is too large for this. Then, open with warm, welcoming comments restating the meeting goals and use that opportunity to thank everyone for being there.

Step 6: Use an Agenda

Not an overly structured one, just a rough guide to keep the group moving from one major point to the next. You can distribute the agenda beforehand—it might help participants prepare—or provide copies at the meeting.

Keep the group moving. Try to develop transition comments or links to move the discussion from point A to point B, and on down the line.

Don't let irrelevancies get a foothold. Politely remind anyone who begins to digress to return to the agenda.

Step 7: Encourage Participation

The brightest members of a group are often reluctant to speak out. Don't shortchange yourself by ignoring them and hearing only from the windbags. Try questioning the quiet types directly: "Can you think of another approach to the problem, Chris?" It could pay off handsomely.

Step 8: Remember: Our Minds Live in Bodies

It's hard to concentrate when we're uncomfortable. Break up long meetings for restroom visits, leg-stretching, and refreshments. And, oh yes, be sure attendees know where the restrooms are.

The meeting site should be comfortable, but not conducive to sleep. The trick here is to avoid extremes. Keep the room cool but not cold. Chairs should be comfortable but firm, lighting adequate but not harsh.

Step 9: Watch for Non-verbal Signs

If you're running the meeting, don't ignore looks of boredom, physical discomfort, disagreement, or agreement. Take appropriate steps by asking the droner to come to the point, announcing a break, calling on the woman who's shaking her head, or testing the group for consensus.

Step 10: Beware of the Signals You Send

If you're whispering to your neighbor, looking out the window, checking your watch, cleaning your nails, or leafing through papers while someone is speaking, you're making a statement, loud and clear: "I don't care what the speaker thinks!"

Step 11: Hone Your Presentation

At your meeting or someone else's, your presentation can determine whether you merely survive or get the results you want. Use solid, reliable information and organize it well. Use plain language. Offer clear conclusions. Make positive recommendations. Use your mind, face, body, and voice to speak with skill and style.

Step 12: End on Time

Better yet, stop early! Our days are scheduled from morning to evening. One meeting that runs over can throw off your entire day. It's no way to create good will.

You'll find it easier to end on time—or early—if you schedule more time than you think you'll need. If you wrap up early, the 10- or 20-minute gift is one your colleagues will appreciate and put to good use.

Sometimes, no matter how hard we try, things take much longer than we anticipate. In the remaining few minutes, arrange a follow-up session to continue the discussion. When you're nearing the end of the allotted time, and the issues haven't been resolved, dismiss the meeting.

Selling Yourself in Negotiations

The dictionary defines the verb *negotiate* as: "to confer with another in bargaining or trade. To hold conference and discussion with a view to reaching agreement on contract." Nowhere does it say that negotiation must involve argument, tantrums, hostility, animosity, or hatred. But unfortunately, that's the meaning management-labor disputes and acrimonious lawsuits have given the word.

Yet, in truth, every time you buy a product, you've negotiated, you've reached agreement on a contract. The dealer put a price tag on his product and you decided to buy it or not. There may be some room for further negotiations over price, terms, time of delivery, and so forth, but in the end you either buy the product or you don't. So ends every negotiation. A decision is made. If it's a good deal for both parties, the negotiation ends successfully. If it isn't a good deal, it doesn't. That's the perfect negotiation. It begins, it ends, and everyone is satisfied that the right decision has been made.

But there are very few opportunities for perfect negotiations left. In most of our everyday transactions, the terms are set with no room for negotiation. And when there is negotiating room, the situation is often turned into a confrontation.

We've already seen that in such adversarial situations, if only one person wins, both lose. In contract talks, in family arguments, in all imperfect negotiation situations, it's vital to realize that if both sides receive fair treatment, both sides come out winners. If you take unfair advantage of the other side in order to win, ultimately, *you* lose.

We All Want to Win

That's become the nature of competition, and from an early age we've learned all kinds of tricks and tactics, some good, some bad, to get what we want.

Among the bad ones are:

- Constant argument, until the other side gives in.
- Aggravation.
- Tantrums.
- Cheating.
- Lying.

Some of the good ones are:

- Logic.
- Analysis.
- Reason.
- Common sense.

And remember that the only successful negotiation is the one in which there are *two winners*. When there are two winners, each comes out with self-esteem intact. No one needs to feel subservient, beaten, put upon, a loser.

Beware of Stress

It's almost inevitable that in imperfect negotiations we develop a lot of stress. Stress is a natural reaction to any out-of-the-ordinary situation, but you mustn't let it dominate you. If you let it take over, it develops into anger, hostility, personal animosity, or even irrational behavior. It controls the negotiation and blocks out logic, reason, and common sense. The possibility of compromise goes down the tube.

When the situation seems to be getting out of hand, when it becomes impossible to like your adversary, when there seems to be absolutely no merit to the other side's point of view, when your adversary seems subhuman to you, when you're tempted to shout and scream, when everything gets personal and seems insulting—take a break for a while.

Call a time-out.

You need a cooling off period.

If you really believe and agree that you're never going to get together, call off the negotiation.

If you do elect to try to keep things going after a break, remember a few simple principles:

- You can't throw a tantrum with your mouth shut.
- You can't scream, yell, or holler when you're smiling.
- You can't fly off the handle with your brows elevated.

Golden Rules of Negotiating

- ▣ Listen.
- ▣ Talk about relevant issues that involve the present.
- ▣ Avoid past problems.
- ▣ Talk about the possible.
- ▣ Avoid the impossible or the unlikely.
- ▣ Start with those issues likely to lend themselves to early solutions.
- ▣ Stick to the agenda items; avoid digressions and detours.
- ▣ If an impasse looks likely, table that issue and move on to the next one.
- ▣ Watch and be alert and sensitive to timing. If you sense the time is right for agenda item number four, skip right to it.

- ☐ Be courteous; avoid put-downs, insults, insinuations, and sarcasm. If you must use humor, make it self-deprecating. Don't make fun of the other guy; be sensitive to his wants and needs.

- ☐ Think and talk alternatives.

- ☐ Think and talk creative solutions. Don't get locked into "doing it this way because that's the way we've always done it."

I have an interesting theory. When it seems impossible to resolve a conflict, when screaming begins, when the other side is dead wrong and you're obviously right (and convinced that even your adversary knows you're right), try *apologizing*. Your overwrought adversary can't. So don't tell the other side it is wrong. It already knows that.

A Positive Beginning

Usually, we start a negotiation with what each side "demands," wants, or expects. I suggest that each side first sift through the other's demands, then go immediately to what's possible.

That seems revolutionary, but it can really cut out a lot of the usual garbage.

Are there any areas of give and take that can serve as the real starting point?

In other words, use the opening moments of a negotiation to sort out the points on the table to find areas of potential agreement rather than start with the areas of extreme disagreement.

Some helpful questions to ask:

- What do we want in common?

- What can we achieve that would put each of us in a somewhat more advantageous position?

- What does each party contribute to the success of the other?

- What can we compromise?

Questions to avoid:

- What can I con them out of?
- What can I do or say to get an edge?
- What can I do to intimidate them?
- What do they owe me?
- How am I superior and how can I flaunt that?
- Don't they realize I can exist without them?
- Why isn't the other side grateful for all I've done for them?

What Are Our Options?

Openly examine the consequences if I give you everything you're asking for. Then turn it around and examine the consequences if you give me everything I want.

A lot of problems can be avoided if we understand how extreme the extremes really are. Then we can move into what solutions might work for both sides if compromise is possible.

A Basic Principle

Some "posturing" may be necessary in your camp or in the opponent's camp in order to keep the "troops" happy, but each of you should be prepared to acknowledge and accept it as part of the negotiating process.

It's remarkable that after a long, acrimonious strike, as the settlement is announced, each side feels obliged to talk about how good the contract is, how happy both sides are with the settlement, and how much this means to everyone involved.

Why, oh why, couldn't they have gotten there before the strike?

A Personal Situation

I vividly remember an adversarial contract negotiation I was involved in many years ago—at least it seemed adversarial to me because I didn't understand that I was part of a "game" being played by two opposing attorneys.

Each side wanted to reach an agreement.

Each side saw great possibilities arising from the proposed relationship.

Many of the details had been hammered out between the attorneys on the telephone before this meeting ever took place. In fact, the contracts were drafted, and supposedly all that remained was for the signing to take place.

My attorney and I flew from New York to Chicago to "finalize" the deal. Three hours after the meeting began, the lawyers were shouting at each other. The final numbers were conflicting. My attorney slammed shut his attaché case, angrily said, "Come on, Arch. We're walking," and stormed out.

I had no idea what I was supposed to do. I'd never been involved in this kind of contract negotiation before. So I felt the tug on my leash and followed. By the time we reached the receptionist's desk, my lawyer winked at me as the other attorneys called us back into the conference room, and we finalized the deal within minutes. It was the "obligatory scene." It was the expected tantrum. It was high drama.

I hope those days of contract negotiations are over, but I fear not. That was the way those particular attorneys felt they were getting an "edge" for their client. I felt all along that the same result could have been reached several hours earlier if the negotiating concept involved what was right for each side. But then again, attorneys are paid by the hour.

Two things to remember:

1. Fair beats unfair.
2. Justice beats injustice.

My attorney admitted to me on the plane ride home that we had achieved exactly what he thought we'd achieve, and he was really proud of having achieved it. That was fine for me, but I wondered how many other deals have been blown away by unnecessary theatrics. I now consider those tactics barbaric.

The notion of courtesy, fairness, and justice should never take second place to a victory that annihilates the "opposition."

Negotiation as Communication

In the ideal negotiation, both sides take turns expressing their ideas and exchanging information. In other words, this is a speaking situation.

Because it is also confrontational, it requires the utmost in speaking skills.

To relax and overcome stress, breathe properly.

To get your points across with honesty and conviction, speak with an open face and appropriate gestures.

Be prepared.

Be confident.

Be courteous.

Be yourself.

Search for ways to be allies rather than enemies.

The statesman seeks solutions.

The general seeks supremacy.

Be a statesman rather than a general.

Selling Your Leadership

Leadership is a word getting a lot of attention these days. It appears in the title of new advice, how-to, and business books with amazing regularity. Definitions abound, but most of the ones I've seen don't help much. It's a totally subjective subject: You think A is a great leader; I like B's style better. As with obscenity, you may not be able to define it, but you know it when you see it.

I've become a serious student of leadership because so many of my clients book me to train leadership groups, or at least have the title "Leadership" on the agenda of the meeting. It's a popular word that doesn't seem to have a consistent meaning or application. It certainly means different things to different people.

So this is my take on the elusive concept:

Years ago, leadership had nothing to do with a specific ability. "Leader" was the title given to the emperor of the organization. It bespoke of POWER. The person was the commandant, the ultimate authority (no questions asked and no quarter given) with complete control. I think of Lee Iacocca, who ruled Chrysler just that way and was then able to bully the government into using public money to bail out his company. It seems that every CEO fell in love with that model and wanted to emulate him. That model has lasted. Today, no one exemplifies this model more than Donald Trump. And there are others who have become celebrities practicing this model. Think of the real person portrayed by Meryl Streep in the film *The Devil Wears Prada*. It was also our perception of Martha Stewart as her employees testified at her trial. It's a leadership quality that still exists, but fortunately there's another way to establish yourself as a leader.

Here's my definition: Leadership is the ability to get others to do what you want, need, or expect them to do, and feel good about doing it. It's the second part (feel good about doing it) that's so elusive.

If I'm in charge, I can certainly demand you do what I expect you to do and insist you get it done. I can give orders. After all, I'm the boss, and everyone knows what that means. It's a sure way to destroy the atmosphere of the workplace.

Today, I believe that approach is on the way out, although it will always be with us. When people hate the boss, sure, the boss is called "leader"—but not a good one, because the followers are an unhappy bunch. If they had another, decent-paying job to go to, they'd be gone in a minute. The expression "good help is hard to find" can be carried over to good leaders.

Here's a list of the qualities I believe it takes to be a good leader:

1. Likable.
2. Trustworthy.
3. Competent and experienced.
4. Part of the team.
5. Able and willing to participate.
6. Ready to listen.
7. Adaptable to change.
8. Eager to share credit.

When we elect a president we're looking for all these qualities, but I've always felt that number one was the crucial factor.

Eisenhower won on the strength of the first three.

Reagan won with far more of number one than his opponent.

Clinton carried the day with one and three, even though he was weak in category two. Dole lost to Clinton because he was so completely out-classed in category one that his strength in two and three simply didn't count enough. I'm sure you've noticed the lack of four through eight in the election analysis. A political campaign is really other-worldly. The other categories are for those of us in the real world.

They're the essential additions that will give your team the pride, the pleasure, and the honor of working with you. Keep the list handy.

The Luck Factor

Defining luck is tricky. It's a hard concept to pin down. It can mean different things to different people.

We all have our own personal experiences with luck. For me, the most memorable began on Christmas Eve in 1944. L Company, 291st Regiment of the 75th Infantry Division was ordered to replace a worn-out cavalry unit in a holding position in the Ardennes Forest outside Manhay, Belgium. The temperature was below freezing and the accumulated snow was more than 3 feet deep over most of the landscape. Incoming artillery and mortar fire made the final hours of the march even more precarious, frightening, and uncomfortable.

The foxholes were already dug, fortunately, but every building that could have provided protection from the elements had been destroyed. Fires were out of the question. There was no relief from the cold and wet of the foxholes and the terrain.

After 10 days of exposure, while I was trying to dry my feet and get into some less wet socks before putting on my wet boots again, I noticed black blisters on each big toe and discoloration developing on all the other toes.

I was sent back to the battalion aid station. It was 2 miles behind our position, and I limped the whole way. The medics took a look at my feet and put me on a cot, and I wasn't allowed to get back on my feet for four months. The diagnosis was severe frostbite. Fortunately, I still have all the parts I arrived with, although my fingers and toes rarely get warm.

Months later, in a letter from the guys who remained with the unit and survived, I was told that the youngster who replaced me in the fox-hole (I was 19, he was 18) was killed the day after I was sent back.

That kind of luck has no logical explanation. That kind of luck is out of control. It's in God's hands. Or it's fate. It's a completely accidental, unexplainable happening.

But that's not the only kind of luck out there, and it's obviously so rare that it's not the kind of luck this chapter is about.

In the musical *Guys and Dolls*, Sky Masterson is about to roll the dice and sings "Luck be a Lady Tonight." It's his plea for a winner.

In *My Fair Lady*, Eliza Doolittle's father, who hasn't earned an honest dollar in his life, sings "With a Little Bit o' Luck" we'll all get by. That's all he needs.

What are some of the different kinds of luck? Our language is full of expressions, including:

- Born lucky.
- Down on his luck.
- Luck of the draw.
- I make my own luck.
- Can't seem to catch a break (no luck).

And there are vastly different ways of looking at the luck life hands you.

"When life hands you lemons [bad luck], make lemonade [change your luck]" was a very popular saying, and I still hear it.

In the poem "Miniver Cheevy," Miniver bemoaned the hand that life dealt him:

> *"Miniver scorned the gold he sought*
> *But sore annoyed was he without it."*

The poem ends:

"Miniver coughed and called it fate;

And kept on drinking."

He never tried to accomplish anything because it was easier to blame failure on bad karma, sad fate, foul luck. Unfortunately, that's not an uncommon attitude.

At the other end of the spectrum are these words of a dying man: "Today I consider myself the luckiest man on the face of the earth." That statement was made by a handsome, gifted, greatly admired baseball star in what was surely the prime of his life, but was forced by an incurable disease to retire from baseball. Lou Gehrig is remembered as much for that statement and the way he faced misfortune as he is for his great career.

It's not necessarily chance that determines your life. What really counts is how you handle the cards that life deals you. You can take life's changes and try to make advantages out of them, or you can let them overwhelm you. Then go ahead and blame bad luck.

Obviously people such as Gehrig and Elizabeth Edwards turned adversity into positive life-affirming situations, and improved the lives of others with their courage.

The dictionary definition of the word *luck* is: "The seemingly chance happening of events which affect one; fortune; lot; fate." People often think of luck as an act of fate, and that's a convenient approach, but that's rarely the whole story. Luck can be not only good or bad, but also good and bad at the same time. The lottery winner is lucky, but often winners' lives are changed in very bad ways they hadn't anticipated, in ways that make them so unhappy that they're miserable for the rest of their lives. We've all read that story in the newspapers of the lottery winner who wishes it had never happened.

Luck is also inconsistent. We hear it called "fickle" all the time. "Lucky at cards, unlucky in love" is so common it's become a cliché. The high of winning big at the casino is almost always followed by the low of losing even more on the next outing. The only certainty about luck is its uncertainty.

My definition of luck is this: getting what you want, making it work for you, and becoming happy.

In the 1950s, Charles Wood was a student at Fordham University in New York. He was a regular on the university's excellent radio station, WFUV. His work was extraordinary and he became very popular among the student body.

After graduation, he got a job on the air at WGMS, Washington, D.C.'s classical music station. While there, he was drafted. Before being scheduled to report to basic training, he was speaking to another WGMS personality who was also the announcer for the United States Army Band. The colleague was finishing his army tour and was soon to be discharged.

Realizing that the band would be looking for a new announcer, Wood lost no time knocking on the door of Major Hugh Curry, the leader of the United States Army Band. He persisted and got the assignment. His entire army career, after basic training, was as the announcer for the band with side jobs as a disc jockey at several area radio stations. Now that's good luck.

After his discharge from the army, he was unsuccessful at getting an on-air broadcasting job anywhere. He accepted a management position at a cable TV station in Hartford. He and the job were not compatible. That was bad luck.

Unemployed and hungry to get back on the air, Wood ran into Frank Maguire, a Fordham classmate who thought Wood was a terrific radio personality and liked him as a person.

As it happened, Maguire was developing and co-producing a brand-new series of radio feature stories for the ABC Radio Network called "Flair Reports." He was looking for personalities who could write an deliver short human interest features and asked Wood to audition.

A nervous, nearly desperate Charles Wood went to the audition, but it was terrible. He could tell that the people in the control room were shaking their heads in disbelief. Fortunately, Maguire remembered how effective his friend had been at Fordham and went against all advice and conventional wisdom, hiring Wood.

There was already a Charles Woods on the union's rolls, which prevented Wood from getting membership under his real name so he used his middle name and became Charles Osgood. He's a brilliant on-air personality with a career that began when someone who could move that career forward found him uniquely qualified and liked him a lot.

(Side note: Maguire also hired a young man who had never been on the air before named Ted Koppel.)

"Down on your luck" means you lose or don't have what you really want or what you deserve but don't get, or watch others get what you think you should have. That's more than just bad luck. It can be frustrating, discouraging, and depressing, making it seem even worse than it is, if you let it eat at you.

Think of luck this way: Good luck is finding gratification in what you get. It's finding happiness that's lasting.

Good luck is having good health.

It's having true friends.

It's loving what you do and doing what you love.

It's being optimistic about the future.

And it's having a loving, happy family.

Luck has been described as being in the right place at the right time. I'll add to that: with the right product (whether that product is an actual object, an idea, or a proposal). Another definition I've always liked is this: the moment when opportunity meets experience and preparedness.

Considered in these terms, luck becomes more than chance or fate. It becomes a part of your life.

In this chapter, I'm approaching luck as an elusive quality, but one that you can help work in your favor. It may sound far-fetched, an impossible daydream, but, yes, I'm suggesting that you can help make your own good luck. I'm suggesting that you focus on using your wits, your contacts, and your written and spoken communication skills in a positive way to get your ideas across. I'm suggesting you use your style, your likability, and your competence to help you get lucky and wind up a winner. I'm suggesting you take matters into your own hands and increase the odds of becoming lucky rather than leaving it to fate.

In Chapter 2, I covered likability. Now I'd like to show you how it's connected with luck.

I've always preached that likability is the key element in winning the job, the promotion, the sale, the election, and the acquittal. If I like you, I welcome you into my life. I may not agree with your ideas, but at least I'll tolerate them. If I don't like you, there's very little chance of developing a positive relationship, regardless of what brilliant ideas you have.

Likability Wins the Job

Of course, there are examples of hiring an unlikable person. Sometimes the applicant pool is empty, and anyone will have to do. Desperation changes any landscape. Sometimes the person thought to be unlikable will work uncommonly hard and uncommonly long hours for uncommonly low pay. These are exceptions to my rule. Normally, likability is the first impression. It's after that first impression that competence comes in to play. Together, likability and competence are an unbeatable combination.

Every job I ever had was offered by a friend who liked me and found me competent, or by an employer who saw those same two qualities and later became my friend.

Ed McMahon and Dick Clark lived in neighboring apartments in a suburban Philadelphia community. Edward R. Murrow was doing a show called *Person to Person* featuring Clark. As was Murrow's custom, he was in a New York studio and the CBS camera crew was on location, this time set up in Clark's apartment. The show went very well, and the owner of the apartment complex gave a party for the CBS personnel, Dick Clark and family, and Chuck Reeves, Clark's producer. Ed was invited and, as often happened, was asked to entertain. (McMahon had lots of experience as an emcee and stand-up comic.) Ed did a turn at the party. Chuck Reeves was impressed and told Ed so. Apparently he filed that performance away in his mind.

One day Reeves, whose office was next door to the office shared by Johnny Carson and his producer, overheard them talking about needing to find a replacement for their announcer on the show *Who Do You Trust?* The announcer had just accepted an offer to do his own show and was leaving.

Reeves called Ed and told him, "Get up here right away and audition." It was a casting call that involved a lot of good people. Apparently Johnny liked Ed's audition, but, when two weeks went by without any word, Ed was convinced that someone else got the job.

Meanwhile, during those two weeks, the McMahon family moved to another suburban Philadelphia community, and Ed had his phone changed and unlisted. Suddenly he was wanted back in New York. The Carson office wanted him but couldn't reach him. The job was his if he could be found soon. Fortunately, Dick Clark knew that Ed's daughter, Claudia, had her own phone. He found the number, called her, and told her to find her father and get him there right away. She was able to reach Ed, and he became the announcer-sidekick on *Who Do You Trust?* When Johnny was offered *The Tonight Show,* he insisted that Ed be part of that package.

It's true that Ed didn't create the opening for announcer on a network television show. It simply came up at that particular time. But he had the background for the job, and had worked a long time honing those particular skills on local shows, entertaining at Veterans Hospitals, on club dates, and at charity benefits. He was ready when the opportunity came. And he was likable. So likable, in fact, that people went out of their way to find him and be sure he got the job. Right place. Right time. Competent. Likable.

Likability Wins the Promotion

The same ground rules apply here. Sure, the person who proves that a 12-hour day is fine and who'll sacrifice family for the job may be promoted.

There are several rule-breakers possible here, but usually the promotion goes to the one who's better liked by the person making the decision.

Lots of promotions go to the "good ol' boy," the golf buddy, the relationship-builder. Nothing says this better than the headline-grabbing Michael Eisner–Mike Ovitz relationship. It was so solid a friendship that it cost Disney huge sums of money when the relationship soured.

One more time: Likability wins the promotion. Them what's liked gets ahead—unless the someone else is the son or daughter or brother-in-law of the person doing the promoting. There's not much you can do about that kind of favoritism. It will always be with us, but there are things you can do to enhance your likability and your competence, and improve your chances for advancement.

Likability Wins the Sale

This concept doesn't need a chapter, a section, or even two paragraphs. It's this simple: When was the last time you bought any big-ticket item from someone you didn't like? It only happens when the price is so ridiculously low that you can't afford to walk away from the deal, but there's no free lunch and, if it seems too good to be true, it probably is.

Likability Wins the Election

My point about likability being the key ingredient of good luck is best illustrated by election outcomes. Every election is decided by the combination of the turnout of the base plus the appeal of the candidate to the undecided voters. I spoke about this in Chapter 1, but it bears repeating here. When the undecided really like one candidate more than the opponent, the likable one wins by a substantial margin. Not many recent elections fall into that category. We have to go as far back as Ronald Reagan for a clear example of this premise. Most elections are decided on a negative basis. The undecided tend to vote for the candidate they dislike less. It doesn't get worse than that. No election made that point more dramatically than the one in the year 2000. Neither George W. Bush nor Al Gore was clearly more likable in the eyes of the undecideds, so that neither man won. We had to have our president given to us by Florida's Secretary of State and the U.S. Supreme Court.

Then in 2004, the election that began with a lot of voters saying "anyone but Bush" ended with many of those people saying "anyone but Bush—but NOT THAT GUY" as they pointed to John Kerry. His lack of likability was self-defeating. I've often wondered if the 2004 election would have come out differently if the Democratic ticket had been reversed with John Edwards as the nominee for president.

During the run-up to the 2008 primaries, Hillary Clinton pointed out that a certain number of voters wouldn't vote for her and a similar number wouldn't vote for anyone else. Her job, she said, was to win over people who hadn't made up their minds. But she never really found the likability key to achieving that goal.

Likability Wins the Acquittal

The courtroom has become the soap opera of the present and the near-future. Once you get hooked, you can't break the habit. Trials have always been great theater. Joan of Arc; Sacco-Vanzetti; the Scopes trial, featuring the all-star cast of Clarence Darrow and William Jennings Bryan; and all the more recent 24/7 celebrity dramas, beginning with O.J. Simpson, Martha Stewart, the Enron and other high-profile business-shenanigan trials, the courtroom wrangling over the custody of Anna Nicole Smith's baby—the list is endless. Nothing else explains the multi-year popularity of the *Law and Order* series on TV.

In any trial, if the evidence is circumstantial with no genuine forensic proof, the verdict will likely be determined by the defendant's likability.

The defense has a tough call in determining whether or not to call the defendant as a witness. The first trial of Frank Quattrone, an early case involving stock-market manipulation, ended in a hung jury. One of the jurors told a reporter that Quattrone would have been acquitted if he *hadn't* testified. Obviously some jurors simply didn't like him.

Conversely, I wondered if the outcomes would have been different had Martha Stewart and "Scooter" Libby been allowed to testify. In the Stewart case, witness after witness for teh prosecution testified about how tough she was, how demanding; she was made out to be a witch. Had she been allowed to show her more "motherly" or "sisterly" side, and present herself as a warm, caring human being, it might have been possible to turn one or more jurors to her side and change the guilty verdict to a mistrial or even an acquittal.

In the Libby trial, plenty of people vouched for him, but the jury never got to see a decent human being.

My advice: If you are the defendant in a trial, be sure to take all the likability training this book offers you, and hire a likable attorney.

A friend who knew I was planning a chapter on luck sent me a series of her favorite quotes. Here they are:

It's hard to detect good luck—it looks so much like something you've earned.

—Frank A. Clark

We must believe in luck. For how else can we explain the success of those we don't like?

—Jean Cocteau

I didn't get old on purpose. It just happened. If you're lucky, it could happen to you.

—Andy Rooney

I'm a lucky guy and I'm happy to be with the Yankees. And I want to thank everyone for making this night necessary.

—Yogi Berra

Depend on a rabbit's foot if you will, but remember it didn't work for the rabbit.

—R.E. Shay

The "Selling Yourself" Handbook

Here is a summary of the major communication skills and techniques that you'll find helpful for a quick review before any speaking assignment. Let's begin with the things I urge you to do.

Throw Out Anything I've Suggested That Isn't Comfortable for You

It's important to appear natural to your audience. If a technique feels fake, it will probably look fake. But before you decide to discard a suggestion, *try it out.* You may find new freedom, new naturalness, and new skill. The open face and the gesture come to mind immediately. You may think you're looking stupid, foolish, and "bug-eyed" when, really, you may be barely elevating those brows. One client told me, "I must never gesture. People are constantly telling me I look like a windmill." I suggested that he continue to use gestures but make a conscious effort to vary them. It worked beautifully for him.

Talk, Chat, Converse, and Communicate

Conversation is the root of all oral communication. The goal of communication is to implant in my mind what's in your mind. And that is done best when you talk to me. The burden of the effort is on the communicator. Don't ever forget that. Moving your mouth and saying words in a common language won't be enough.

Work at Getting Your Ideas Across

Again, this is the difference between the "good morning" of small talk and the "good morning" that sounds genuine. It takes an extra effort. Make that effort.

Be Yourself

The real you is far more desirable for an audience than the one you think you're supposed to be. Carefully watch the young man who's making a presentation to an audience of successful businesspeople. He's probably going to do exactly the wrong things: try to impress them with his maturity and professionalism rather than to express his ideas clearly, concisely, and simply. You, speaking naturally and with good preparation, are the most impressive person you can be.

Open Your Face

The open face is the strongest signal an audience can receive that there's warmth, affection, and love motivating the communicator. No body language, no non-verbal communication technique does what the open face does. It's the skill that pays the quickest dividends in audience acceptance.

Smile When Appropriate and Genuine

Just as you can't pout or throw a tantrum with your brows elevated, you can't look angry, hateful, or oppressive when there's a real, honest-to-goodness smile on your face. It's another wonderful signal of genuine affection, and we can't ever get too much of that.

Gesture When It's Comfortable and Appropriate

Nothing reaches across the distance between you and your audience the way a gesture does. Nothing serves as well as a hug without touching. The gesture is the speaker's picture-painting device. It illustrates and emphasizes what you're saying. It demonstrates, so your gestures should be reserved for the highly descriptive words and the strong action words. The open face and the gesture are the two techniques that make the most profound difference in a speaker's acceptance and enjoyment by an audience.

Be Open, Giving, Warm, Friendly, and Loving

All the other suggestions are wrapped up into this one. When you love your audience, the audience loves you back. That's when communication is at its purest and most perfect. The audience concentrates exclusively on the message it's getting. Again, remember the baby: It doesn't understand your words, but your love sends the perfect signals, and the message is complete.

Speak in a Quiet, Conversational Voice

This really takes work and concentration until it becomes a habit. A loud voice is a turn-off. It's only successful with young people and their music. Otherwise, loud is offensive. Soft is soothing, comforting, and satisfying.

Pause

Trust your audience. They'll wait for you if your pause is effective. It will even heighten their understanding of your message. Don't move your mouth until your mind is in high gear. The pause gives you a chance to think clearly so that what you say will be the best message you can deliver at that moment.

Think Silently

Nothing is more frustrating...uh...than the...uh...person who...uh...never gets to the...uh...end.

Stay Calm and Reasonable

Nothing is more embarrassing than being in the presence of two people who are screaming at each other. Neither wins your support or your sympathy. The one who appears to be reasonable and sensible, and is trying to be reassuring usually wins. Let it be you.

Be Positive

Just about everyone prefers a "can do" person to a "no can do" one. Also, you can stay out of a lot of trouble by giving information rather than issuing denials and being negative and defensive.

Talk With Pride

What a difference pride makes in your attitude and your delivery! Think of the attitude that follows the statements "I'm proud to be able to tell you," or "Our record speaks for itself. It's the best in our field," as opposed to "We never do that," or "You don't have your facts straight."

Be Ready for the Worst Possible Scenario

Be prepared for confrontation. And when someone fires at you, don't immediately fire back. You'll miss unless you pause, look directly at your adversary, think carefully about your reply, and then give a positive answer rather than a defensive reply or a denial. With the possible exception of "when did you stop beating your wife?" almost any question or accusation can be turned in your favor.

Be Honest

Yes, there are some people who can lie effectively, but you and I aren't among them. Yes, the truth can be a cause for trouble, but if you tell the truth, you never have to remember what you said. You can never get in as much trouble as the trouble that can be caused by lying. If you can't tell the truth, keep your mouth shut, even if people suspect you may be hiding something. The fact is that people love to be told the truth, even if the teller knows he's doing some damage to himself.

Admit "I Don't Know"

It's a key provision of honesty. No one expects you to know everything, but each of us feels "I should know the answer to that," and so we blurt out an answer. Any answer is likely to be either wrong or a lie when you really don't know.

Admit "I Don't Understand Your Question"

This is another key to honesty that's harder to accomplish than it sounds. People think they'll appear dumb if they admit to not understanding a question. You'll look even dumber if you give a wrong or inept answer.

Remember Your Audience at All Times

A speaker is not a speaker without an audience. And if an audience likes what they see and hear, understands you, agrees with you, trusts and believes you, you can be a winner.

Keep Eye Contact

You're here for your audience. Talk to them. Involve them. When you look at objects instead of people, people grow uninterested if not downright bored. When you look up, you look as if you're asking God for a cue card. When you look down, it appears that you're looking for help from your shoes. Side-to-side movement looks shifty-eyed. Random eye movement suggests fear and uncertainty. Strong eye contact suggests confidence and control. Simply put: Eye contact is your connection to the audience.

Concentrate on What You Know

You have good information. What you need is time to think about just what that information is and how you can get it across with the greatest impact.

You're the Expert

That's the reason you're speaking. You have no cause to feel self-conscious unless you're asked to speak on a subject about which you have very little, insufficient, or no information. In that case, decline, admitting that this is not your area of expertise.

Have Confidence in Your Preparation, Your Style, and Your Speaking Skills

Fear is your worst enemy. Practicing and using all the speaking skills we have talked about will help you convert crippling fear into energy-producing confidence.

Organize Your Material

Give your audience the benefit of forethought—prepare. They deserve it. Decide what method of preparation works best for you: outline, notes, or manuscript. Take the time to do it right.

Practice Aloud

Use recorders, friends, colleagues, a mirror, or a video recorder if it's available. It will help you monitor yourself to make sure you're using the techniques you've learned here and to give a dynamite presentation.

Use Your Text Properly

Prepare the words on the paper, using large type and wide margins. Get rid of paper clips and staples. Put your pages in the right order before you get to your feet.

Use Simple Language

Don't obfuscate. Don't prevaricate. Don't even prioritize in front of a group.

Use Short Sentences

Ideas with few words are memorable. They're clear and understandable. Nobody likes a windbag.

Be Concise

If you can say it in five words, you shouldn't use 50. Some sentences that can't be improved on are "I love you," "They won," "It's a boy," "You're hired," "Good job," and "I'll take it." And as an added bonus, remember this when you're writing letters, proposals, and memos. It works.

Be Clear

Figure out how to say what you mean and mean what you say; then do it. Make your sentences as simple, direct, and easy-to-understand as you can. Far too often people say to other people, "That's not what you said." Often it *was* what was said, but it wasn't said the best possible way for understanding.

Edit Yourself

When you think you're finished preparing, cut, then cut some more. Leave your audience wishing you'd said more rather than wondering why you didn't end half an hour earlier. Don't be the big snooze. Don't try to tell them everything you know. They don't want to hear it.

Express Yourself

Deliver the material in the most dynamic way you can. Stop trying to impress an audience with your body of knowledge. Impress them with how beautifully you deliver your ideas.

Practice the Rhythm of Eye Contact

Your mouth should never be moving while your eyes are looking at the page, the floor, or the back wall. As the words flow out, your eyes should be on your audience. Even speakers who know and understand this important principle find that bad habits, fear of losing their place, and fear of the pause cause them to look down toward the paper as they approach the last words of a sentence and to say the first word or two of the next sentence while their eyes are still down. It takes a lot of practice to master this technique because we've been doing it wrong for all the years we've been speaking.

Communicate Ideas

One of the hardest traps to overcome is to stop reading words when there's a text in front of you. From now on, stop trying to get exact words from the page. Deliver ideas. Your audience wants to hear what's on your mind, not what's on a piece of paper.

Be Attentive to Your Audience's Signals

Just as everything you say and do sends signals to your audience, they're sending you signals all the time. If you see that you're losing them, don't panic. That only makes the situation worse for everyone. Stay calm. If you're far along, it's probably best to wrap it up. If you're at the early part, pull back, concentrate harder on the open face and the gesture, and put more effort into the concept of making intellectual love to your audience. Don't speed up; that's deadly. It tells your audience you want to get it over with. Be more deliberate and offer them more of you. Remember that no one has the right to be dull. When it's all over and you've had a chance to recover, try to analyze why you lost their attention so it doesn't happen the next time you have to speak.

Practice Diaphragmatic Breathing

It's both a speaking tool and a longevity tool. It helps you convert stress into energy. The diaphragm moves out slightly on the inhalation and back in on the exhalation. Remember it. Practice it. It may help keep a heart attack or a stroke from claiming you too soon. It will certainly help you become a more relaxed and natural speaker.

Look and Sound Pleasant and Interesting

The audience has arrived predisposed to like you. Don't turn that around by giving them a reason to tune you out.

Send Positive, Loving Signals

When in doubt, remember again what you do when you speak to a baby. The signals are always right. Use them on an adult audience. Until you're willing to make a fool of yourself in front of an audience, you will.

Be Likable

The winner is the person we like. The official who gets elected is the one we like. The likable speaker is the one we believe.

∎∎∎

And for every "do" in the previous list, there's a corresponding "don't" in the following:

- ▣ Don't use any of my advice if it doesn't seem natural for you.
- ▣ Don't make a speech, preach, teach, orate, or pontificate.
- ▣ Don't imitate anyone else.
- ▣ Don't frown (closed face) or look dead (neutral face).
- ▣ Don't hide or tie up your hands.
- ▣ Don't shout or try to reach the back wall.
- ▣ Don't run on at the mouth.
- ▣ Don't use sounds to think by. Get rid of all audible pauses.
- ▣ Don't get angry or uptight.

- Don't repeat or reinforce negatives.

- Don't be defensive.

- Don't wing it.

- Don't lie or make it up as you go along.

- Don't try to give an answer if you don't understand the question or if you don't know the answer.

- Don't repeat a nasty question or ask the questioner to repeat the question.

- Don't think about your adversary or yourself.

- Don't think "down" or "up" or "away."

- Don't assume your audience knows your message.

- Don't worry about being too simple.

- Don't consider your material dull.

- Don't wait until the last minute to prepare.

- Don't try to intellectualize everything.

- Don't spin your wheels or waste time.

- Don't complicate your text.

- Don't tell your audience everything you know.

- Don't hide behind obscure, technical language.

- Don't show off your brilliance.

- Don't try to impress the audience.

- Don't deliver your talk to your script, the lectern, or your slides.

- Don't read words to your audience.

- Don't distract or be blatant in speech or dress.

- Don't ignore the audience's needs, expectations, or wants.

What your audience needs, expects, and wants is you, *so be yourself.*

Appendix

Lustberg on the Open Face

1. You achieve the open face by raising your eyebrows, creating horizontal lines in your forehead, and holding the position for a short time.

2. The open face is the most likable expression.

3. You look your most attractive when you open your face and smile.

4. A smile is sometimes inappropriate, but an open face always works.

5. An open face makes you look confident and self-assured.

6. It makes you look honest and believable.

7. When you're having fun, you open your face naturally.

8. When you're under stress, you have to remember to open your face.

9. Draw a small open face on your text or notes as a reminder.

10. It's almost impossible not to open your face when you talk to a baby.

11. An open face says, "I care."

12. An open face says, "I want us to understand each other."

13. An open face adds music to your voice.

14. We can hear the warmth of an open face on the radio, on tape, and over the phone.

Lustberg on Mistakes in Preparing and Delivering Presentations

1. Trying to compose a great work of literature.

2. Overwhelming the audience with statistics, charts, graphs, overheads, slides, and other unmemorable information.

3. Letting someone else write your material and then not working on it until the last minute.

4. Burying your nose in the text and reading a tedious group of words to an audience that is either leaving or falling asleep.

5. Forgetting that your appearance is an opportunity to communicate, not an exercise in boredom.

6. Believing that quantity is an acceptable substitute for quality.

7. Failing to personalize and individualize the message.

8. Not practicing the presentation aloud until it feels natural and comfortable.

9. Trying to impress the audience with your knowledge, professionalism, or authority in order to prove your competence.

10. Talking around the subject, or overstating or disguising the truth for effect.

11. Knocking other people and other views rather than thoroughly showing the merits of your message.

12. Failing to acknowledge problems or the perception of problems in the minds of listeners.

13. Taking the audience and its interest in you and your subject for granted.

14. Winging it.

15. Allowing yourself to be dull by convincing yourself that the material is dull.

16. Trying to tell the audience everything you know.

17. Presenting with a closed or neutral face.

18. Tying up your hands, making gesture impossible.

19. Not knowing how or when to stop.

20. Failing to create a vivid opening and a blockbuster closing.

Lustberg on Solid Communication

Conversation is the root of all oral communication. The goal of communication is to implant in my mind what's in your mind. And that is done best when you talk to me. The burden of the effort is on the communicator. Don't ever forget that. Moving your mouth and saying words in a common language won't be enough. The one who appears to be reasonable and sensible, and who tries to be reassuring usually wins. *Let it be you.*

This book is designed to help you become an effective communicator—a winner.

Remember that your goal is to be liked. You want to win over the people in your audience. Think of *60 Minutes*.

When the person being interviewed looks shady, evasive, or unlikable, you root for the interviewer. You want him to burst that awful person's balloon. When the person he's interviewing looks pleasant, likable, and in control, you tend to wonder why he's so rotten to that nice person.

Use my techniques to make yourself that likable person everyone is rooting for. And remember: Practice makes perfect.

Practice with your colleagues, your family, your neighbors, and your coworkers. See how warmly people react to the smile, the open face, the gesture, and the eye contact. Put your new skills to work the next time you meet a stranger. Open your face, smile, and say, "Good morning!" You'll probably make that stranger's day. You'll probably get such a pleasant response, you'll make your own day, too.

When you're called upon to speak, make it a point to be the same human being you are when you talk to your neighbors and friends. Don't be surprised when you're met with equal warmth and enthusiasm!

Lustberg on Points to Remember

Your mind:

- Know in advance exactly what you can—and cannot—say about the organization you represent.

- Develop a positive attitude and frame of mind. Maintain it no matter what.

- Eliminate negative buzzwords.

- Make positive statements. Tell people what you *do,* not what you *don't do.*

- Pause. Don't talk until your mind is working.

- Maintain a sense of rapport with the person you're talking to.

- Make your point in terms that are meaningful and memorable.

- Relax. Breathe correctly.

- Keep it short and simple.

Your face:

- Don't frown or put on a neutral mask in an effort to look professional. Instead, raise your brows to project a warm, welcoming person.

- Smile at every appropriate opportunity.

Your body:

- Stand comfortably but erect.

- If you're seated, keep your back straight and lean slightly forward.

- Force yourself to use gestures—but only when they look natural.

Your voice:

- Make your tone warm by opening up your face and using gestures.

- Use pitch and rate conversationally.

- Use only enough volume to be heard.

Lustberg on a Checklist Before Testifying

Remember your mission:

- Have you learned everything you can about your audience?

- Have you prepared two texts (one detailed, one abbreviated)?

- Have you put into your own words any material from other experts?

Remember what's expected of you:

- Make your points concisely and coherently.

- Be positive.

- Pay attention to protocol.

Remember persuasion:

- Your audience is divided into three groups: for you, against you, and undecided (talk to them).

- Do you know the issue?

- Do you know the other side's position, arguments?

- Have you rehearsed your presentation?

Is your testimony:

- Simple?
- Well-organized?
- Well-constructed?
- Persuasive?
- Colorful?
- Brief?
- Well-documented?
- Logical?
- Positive?
- Quotable?

Remember basic testimony information:

- Your name, title, and affiliation.
- Your background (to establish credibility).
- Who you're representing.
- The legislation or issue.
- Areas of consideration.
- Your position or argument.
- What you'd like to see accomplished.

Lustberg on a Winning Media Interview

- **Prepare.** Get together with your team and throw the toughest curveballs you can at one another. Practice, practice, practice.

- **Pause.** Stop and think before you speak. A second or two might feel awkward to you, but your audience welcomes a moment to think about what's just been said.

- **Remain silent.** Keep quiet in the...uh...y'know...the...uh, uh...pause...know what I mean?

- **Inform.** Your job in an interview is to give information.

- **Don't speak off the record.** If you don't want to see it in print, hear it on the radio, or watch it repeated on television, *don't say it*.

- **Be honest.** If there's a problem, acknowledge it. Admit it if you don't know the answer.

- **Be the voice of reason.** Getting angry, losing your cool, or taking an attack personally plays right into the tabloid reporter's hands. It makes good copy—for everyone but you.

- **Be positive.** Instead of using "didn't," "don't," or "won't," tell us what you did, do, or will do.

- **Beware of the buzzword trap.** Don't blurt out a denial. Tell a story that relevantly contradicts the error.

- **Be simple.** Get rid of jargon and deliver conversation, not literature. Remember Churchill: "Short words are the best, and short words, when old, are best of all."

- **Be proud.** If you've done something good, tell us.

- **Maintain eye contact.** When your eyes are all over the place, it's hard to like you or trust you. Look at your interviewer as you speak.

- **Open your face—raise those eyebrows—show your eyes.** It's an expression that says, "I care."

- **Smile when it's appropriate and genuine.** It says, "I like you."

- **Gesture.** It's the communicator's equivalent of a hug. It shows you really want your audience to share your message.

- **Be memorable.** Use stories, anecdotes, examples, similes, and metaphors. Paint word pictures.

- **Personalize.** Involve your audience.

Lustberg on Speaker Tips

Be yourself:

- Speak in a quiet, conversational voice.
- Talk, chat, converse, and communicate.
- Work at getting your ideas across.
- Smile when appropriate and genuine.
- Gesture when it's comfortable and appropriate.
- Be open, giving, warm, friendly, and loving.
- Express yourself. Forget about impressing your listener.

Prepare:

- Organize your material.
- Be concise.
- Use simple language. Use short sentences.
- Look and sound pleasant.
- Send positive, loving signals.
- Be attentive to your audience's signals.

Have confidence:

- In your preparation, your style, your speaking skill.
- Be positive. Talk with pride. Be honest.
- Be ready for the worst possible scenario.
- Admit "I don't know," or "I don't understand your question."
- Concentrate on what you do know.
- You're the expert.

Remember:

- Open your face.
- Pause. Think silently. Stay calm and reasonable.

- Your audience wants you to succeed.
- Be likable.

Lustberg on Choosing the Right Word

Use the active voice:

- *Change:* "It was decided by Congress...."

  To: "Congress decided...."

- *Change:* "It is incumbent upon our industry to ensure...."

  To: "We have to...."

- *Change:* "The language capabilities and challenges facing every child, including those who are learning English as a second language, must be carefully considered as we plan experiences and instruction."

  To: "As we plan, we must carefully consider the language capabilities and challenges of every child."

Use simple, everyday language:

- *Change:* "...obviously, however, it is not enough simply to set forth a shared vision."

  To: "...but a shared vision isn't enough."

- *Change:* "...develop data to demonstrate the correlation between laboratory test results and field performance."

  To: "...test lab results in the real world."

- *Change:* "...accordingly, students need to read and study literary texts in a variety of genres, including poetry, short stories, novels, plays, essays, and biographies."

  To: "...so students should read and study all kinds of literature."

- *Change:* "...throughout the past decade."

  To: "...for 10 years."

Use as few words as possible:

- *Change:* "Individuals who are competent at communicating with others are sensitive to the needs of different audiences."

  To: "Good communicators know different audiences have different needs."

- *Change:* "visual diagrams."

  To: "diagrams."

- *Change:* "the positive as well as the negative."

  To: "the good and the bad."

Use contractions:

- *Change:* "We will not...."

  To: "We won't...."

- *Change:* "That, quite frankly, is tragic."

  To: "That's tragic."

Be positive:

- *Change:* "We are not just standing by and watching."

  To: "We're joining in."

- *Change:* "It is not difficult to comprehend."

  To: "It's easy to understand."

- *Change:* "Knowing how to learn has not often been highlighted explicitly as part of instructional content in the English language arts."

  To: "Teaching how to learn is rarely seen as part of teaching English."

Be specific:

- *Change:* "Educator."

  To: "Teacher" or "professor" or "coach" or "trainer."

- *Change:* "Facility."

  To: "School" or "hospital" or "factory" or "prison."

- *Change:* "Legislative initiative."

  To: "Law" or "regulation."

Break up long, complex sentences:

- *Change:* "Literary works are valuable not just as informative or communicative vehicles, but as artistic creations and representations of human culture at particular times and in particular places."

  To: "Literature is valuable, not just as information, but as art. It represents the human culture of a certain place and time."

■■■

No one can follow all these rules all the time, but the closer you get, the better you'll be at getting your message across.

A Final Word

Shakespeare taught the ultimate classical course in public speaking in Hamlet's "Advice to the Players" speech. Hamlet says:

> Speak the speech, I pray you, as I pronounced it to you, trippingly on the tongue. But if you mouth it, as many of our players do, I had as lief the town crier spoke my lines. Nor do not saw the air too much with your hand, thus, but use all gently, for in the very torrent, tempest, and (as I may say) whirlwind of your passion, you must acquire and beget a temperance that may give it smoothness. O, it offends me to the soul to hear a robustious periwig-pated fellow tear a passion to tatters, to very rags, to

split the ears of the groundlings, who for the most part are capable of nothing but inexplicable dumb shows and noise. I would have such a fellow whipped for o'erdoing Termagant. It out-herods Herod. Pray you avoid it.

Be not too tame neither, but let your own discretion be your tutor. Suit the action to the word, the word to the action, with this special observance, that you o'erstep not the modesty of nature. For anything so overdone is from the purpose of playing, whose end, both at the first and now, was and is, to hold, as 'twere, the mirror up to nature, to show virtue her own feature, scorn her own image, and the very age and body of the time his form and pressure. Now this overdone, or come tardy off, though it make the unskillful laugh, cannot but make the judicious grieve, the censure of the which one must in your allowance o'erweigh a whole theatre of others. O, there have been players that I have seen play, and heard others praise, and that highly, (not to speak profanely), that neither having th' accent of Christians, nor the gait of Christian, pagan, nor man, have so strutted and bellowed that I have thought some of Nature's journeymen had made men, and not made them well, they imitated humanity so abominably.

Reform it altogether! And let those that play your clowns speak no more than is set down for them, for there be of them that will themselves laugh, to set on some quantity of barren spectators to laugh too, though in the mean time some necessary question the play be then to be considered: that's villainous and

shows a most pitiful ambition in the fool that uses it.
Go make you ready.

Nothing summarizes my training and the contents of this book better than an ancient proverb:

Tell me and I'll forget.

Show me and I may remember.

Involve me and I'll understand.

Index

About the Author

Charles Osgood of CBS saw Arch Lustberg at a presentation for the Nevada Governor's Conference on Tourism and wrote:

> "Arch has taught the art of effective communications to powerful leaders in government and industry. He's one of the best public speakers I've ever heard. He's bright, witty, engaging, and entertaining. Nobody does it better."

Lustberg's career has been unique and intriguing. He taught speech and drama at the Catholic University of America in Washington, D.C., for 10 years.

When he left academe, he co-produced the Tony Award–nominated musical *Don't Bother Me, I Can't Cope*. He then co-produced the off-Broadway Outer Critics Circle Award–winning revue *Tuscaloosa's Calling Me, But I'm Not Going*.

He produced and directed many record albums in the days of the LP, most notably Grammy Award–winning "Gallant Men" by the late Senator Everett McKinley Dirksen, and *The Voice of the People*, a dramatized history of the U.S. Capitol Building, which starred Helen Hayes and E.G. Marshall.

Lustberg directed the United States Chamber of Commerce Communicator workshops, training elected officials, business leaders, association executives, and professionals in every field, prior to opening his own business, Arch Lustberg Communications.

His client list is a who's who of business.

In this book, Lustberg shares his techniques on the art of spoken communications with you.

His quarterly newsletter, *The Lustberg Communicator*, is available at no charge on his Website (*www.lustberg.net*), where you'll find lots of helpful hints. To receive his commentaries on current speaking topics, send your e-mail address to lustberg@erols.com, and you'll receive topical updates involving his observations on political campaigns, major speeches, and relevant communication subjects.